THE

TAO

OF

WU

RIVERHEAD BOOKS

a member of Penguin Group (USA) Inc.

New York

2009

THE
TAO
OF
WU

The RZA

WITH CHRIS NORRIS

RIVERHEAD BOOKS
Published by the Penguin Group
Penguin Group (USA) Inc., 375 Hudson Street, New York, New York 10014, USA ·
Penguin Group (Canada), 90 Eglinton Avenue East, Suite 700, Toronto, Ontario M4P
2Y3, Canada (a division of Pearson Penguin Canada Inc.) · Penguin Books Ltd,
80 Strand, London WC2R 0RL, England · Penguin Ireland, 25 St Stephen's Green,
Dublin 2, Ireland (a division of Penguin Books Ltd) · Penguin Group (Australia), 250
Camberwell Road, Camberwell, Victoria 3124, Australia (a division of
Pearson Australia Group Pty Ltd) · Penguin Books India Pvt Ltd,
11 Community Centre, Panchsheel Park, New Delhi–110 017, India · Penguin Group
(NZ), 67 Apollo Drive, Rosedale, North Shore 0632, New Zealand
(a division of Pearson New Zealand Ltd) · Penguin Books (South Africa)
(Pty) Ltd, 24 Sturdee Avenue, Rosebank, Johannesburg 2196, South Africa

Penguin Books Ltd, Registered Offices: 80 Strand, London WC2R 0RL, England

Library of Congress Cataloging-in-Publication Data

RZA (Rapper).
The Tao of Wu / the RZA, with Chris Norris.
p.   cm.
ISBN 978-1-59448-885-6
1. RZA (Rapper).   2. Rap musicians—United States—Biography.
I. Norris, Chris.   II. Title.
ML420.R984A3   2009   2009030866
782.421649092—dc22
[B]

Printed in the United States of America
1   3   5   7   9   10   8   6   4   2

BOOK DESIGN BY MEIGHAN CAVANAUGH

While the author has made every effort to provide accurate telephone numbers and
Internet addresses at the time of publication, neither the publisher nor the author
assumes any responsibility for errors, or for changes that occur after publication.
Further, the publisher does not have any control over and does not assume any
responsibility for author or third-party websites or their content.

FOREWORD

by Sifu Shi Yan Ming

Amituofo.

I congratulate the world for this beautiful gift, wisdom from the life and travels of RZA, wisdom I truly believe draws from the deepest pools of human thought and spirit.

I was born in China's Henan Province, and when I was five years old, my parents left me at the Shaolin temple. There, I grew up and became the most handsome of the thirty-fourth generation of Shaolin warrior monks, the world's oldest practitioners of the Cha'an Buddhist philosophy and martial art known as kung fu. In 1992, on a Shaolin U.S. tour, I defected to the United States to share Shaolin wisdom with the world. With no money, no possessions, and no English, I made my way from San Francisco to New York, where I founded the USA Shaolin temple. Not long after that, I met the RZA, whose life I found very similar to my own. In fact, I felt I had known him forever.

We met in 1995, at a party for the release of *Liquid Swords*. RZA was dressed very simply, but when we were introduced, I could feel a profound presence. To a Cha'an Buddhist, wisdom is expressed in the physical as well as the mental—there's no difference—and it's the same with the RZA. You feel his wisdom in what he says, how he stands, how he moves. We shook hands and hugged—like a hip-hop hug—and began to talk.

At that time I didn't know much English—and he speaks very fast—but, as strange as this sounds, I completely understood what he was saying. We talked about the Shaolin temple's history and philosophy, and I was very impressed with his knowledge. We talked about music, film, and science, and I could feel such understanding, such intelligence. I had met many Americans by this time, but the RZA was different. He was American—born in the United States—but he had truly absorbed Buddhist and Taoist philosophies in his own way, with an open mind and an open heart. That's how we communicated then—mind-to-mind, heart-to-heart—and it's how we communicate to this day.

I travel to many countries, meet many people from around the world, but most of them cannot have that kind of open mind and open heart. A lot of people think that if they believe in Buddha, they cannot go to church. If they believe in Muhammad, they cannot be in a monastery. But there's no difference. *You* are the monastery—always, wherever you are—and this is something the RZA has understood for a long, long time.

Before I met him, I mostly listened to Buddhist music. Now I listen to the Wu-Tang Clan every chance I get. (Whasup! Represent!) Wu-Tang is known as the most famous group ever to practice rap as a martial art, which, in the RZA's case, happens to be the absolute truth. In kung fu, martial art and philosophy are the same, no difference. When the RZA makes music, it's just like that—his philosophy and music are as one. Some of his sounds and lyrics might seem simple, but they're not. He's a very funny guy, but his understanding is also very deep. And even when he's not making music, that philosophy is in everything he says and does—like a true Cha'an Buddhist.

In Buddhism, the highest and most valuable number is seven. When a wise monk passes away, the monastery builds a pagoda in his memory. Some pagodas get one floor, some get two or three. But if the man was known as the wisest and most enlightened of all monks, his pagoda gets seven. I believe the seven pillars of wisdom in this book are like the seven floors of an exalted monk's pagoda. They represent the wisdom, knowledge, and enlightenment of a soul that has never stopped training, never stopped learning.

At my temple, I give my disciples, students, and followers around the world a few basic messages: (1) Life is beautiful; (2) More Chi! Train harder! (3) Be honest with yourself and be honest with others; (4) Respect yourself, respect others; (5) 100% express your beautiful life. When the RZA began studying with me, I never had to tell him this. He already knew.

In case you're wondering, *How is his kung fu?* Fantastic! Beautiful! How could it be otherwise? He's the RZA: different from the others. His spirit drives his actions, and those actions change the world.

Amituofo,
Sifu Shi Yan Ming
Founder and Abbot of the USA Shaolin Temple
New York City, 2009

All Praise due to Allah, Lord of all the Worlds.

*Supreme Peace and Blessing. This Book of Wisdom is Volume
Two of the Wu-Tang Manual and a second installment to the
chambers of ideas of the Wu-Tang as told by the Abbot.*

*In the Divine Mathematics, Knowledge is 1: the foundation of
all things. Wisdom is 2: the manifestation of Knowledge. It is
knowledge in action. Manifestation = Man Fest = Speak Action
is action.*

*Wisdom is the separation that begins life. It is the explosion
that created the universe. It is the division of every cell that
multiplies to form a single life. It is the partition God renders
when he says, "Let there be Light"—separating light from dark,
sky from ocean. It is the detachment of man from his rib to
create woman.*

*Wisdom is woman. It is the womb one must pass through to
become mentally born. Knowledge and Wisdom give birth to
Understanding just as man and woman give birth to a child.*

*Wisdom is the word. It is the way to make Knowledge known.
"In the beginning was the Word and the Word was with God
and the word became flesh." God's Knowledge was made
manifest through words to create life.*

Wisdom is reflection in time. Knowledge is static and timeless. It is the moment before the Big Bang, the explosion brings and borns Understanding through the fourth dimension, which is time.

Wisdom is water. It is the flood that drowned the wicked in the time of Noah. It is the sea that drowned the Pharaoh's army when Moses used it to part the waters. It is the universal solvent into which all things dissolve in time.

WISDOM *n.*

1: the effectual mediating principle or personification of God's will in the creation of the world . . . 2a(1): accumulated information: philosophic or scientific learning . . . (2): accumulated lore or instinctive adaptation . . . b: the intelligent application of learning : ability to discern inner qualities and essential relationships . . . 3a: an embodiment of wisdom . . . b: a wise attitude or course of action . . . c: a person of superior intellectual attainments . . . 4: the teachings of the ancient wise men (as of Babylon, Egypt, or Palestine) relating to the art of living and sometimes to philosophical problems concerning the universe, man, or God and forming a class of literature represented in the Hebrew books of Job, Proverbs, Ecclesiastes, Ecclesiasticus, and the Wisdom of Solomon

—*Webster's Dictionary*, Third New International Edition

THE
TAO
OF
WU

The journey of a thousand miles
begins with a single step.

—Lao-tzu

If you live in the projects, you don't leave them much. Everything is right there: laundry, grocery store, check-cashing place—all set up so you can live your whole life in a four-block radius. I've lived in at least ten different projects in New York—Van Dyke in Brownsville, Marcus Garvey in East New York, Park Hill and Stapleton in Staten Island—and they all taught me something, even if they were lessons no one would choose.

Imagine you're eight years old, going to the store with thirty-five cents to buy a pack of Now and Laters and a bag of sunflower seeds. You get there, three teenagers choke you with an umbrella, take your thirty-five cents, and buy cigarettes. That's the projects—math and economics class on every block. Imagine you live with eighteen relatives in a two-bedroom apartment across the street from the courthouse and county jail. You wonder why the jail and courthouse are so close to the projects; when you get locked up there a few years later, you learn. You learn civics, government, law, and science every day—especially science. Because the projects, like jail, is a science project. One no one expects you to leave.

I did leave—moved out of Stapleton projects at twenty-three, in 1992—and not long after that, my brothers in the Wu-Tang Clan and I became citizens of the world. But those project lessons are still with all of us, one of the foundations for wisdom. They're the darkness that lets us see light.

I'll give you an example.

In 1978, my mother, who worked in a numbers house, hit the number for about four g's—enough money to move eight of us into a three-bedroom place on Dumont Avenue. This was in Marcus Garvey, a violent ghetto, but for a minute there we felt like the white kids on the TV show *Eight Is Enough*: eight kids with toys, bikes, and a new home. But before we could move in, the place was robbed. All our stuff—toys, bikes, furniture—was gone, right before Christmas. We were heartbroken but moved in anyway, and before long I got to know our next-door neighbor, Chili-Wop.

Chili-Wop was the coolest motherfucker you'd ever meet. He was a drug dealer with muscles, gold chains, mad style, and a crazy way of talking. "Whasuuup!" he'd yell. "It's Chili-Waaawp, nigga, whaaaat!" For some reason, Chili-Wop took a liking to me. He started taking me on trips—drug runs, really, although I didn't know it at the time—and began looking out for me. Chili-Wop became an ally, a protector in a violent world. Finally, after I'd lived there for nearly two years, he told me something. "When y'all first moved in, I robbed your house, maaan. I never knew you was gonna be a cool family." When he told me, there wasn't much I could do about it, and by then he was like my best friend—or as they say in the hood nowadays, my big homie—so in a way it was cool.

That's just one hood lesson: Your allies can arrive as enemies, blessings as a curse.

When I was ten, Chili-Wop was sixteen. By the time I was eleven, Chili-Wop's crew was shot up by rival drug dealers, and he ended up in jail. That was life on Dumont Avenue, which I now see for what it was: hell—a hell of violence, addiction, misery, and humiliation. These forces were in even the air and water; in times of heavy rain, human excrement floated by under our basement-level bedroom, where me and my five brothers slept on two twin beds. No one chooses to live like that, but I now see that even that experience—living where shit floats—was a source of precious wisdom.

It's like a story from the life of Da'Mo, the Indian monk

who brought Zen Buddhism to China. One day, Da'Mo was talking with another monk, who began to denounce mud—saying how dirty it was, how a man should stay clean, keep away from mud. But Da'Mo observed that the lotus grows on mud: "How can you defame mud when such a beautiful flower grows from it?" he asked. Da'Mo's teachings reached everywhere—from the samurai class of Japan to the kung fu monks of Shaolin to the housing projects of Staten Island. I apply Da'Mo's wisdom to the projects. I believe the misery there brought forth a certain flower that wouldn't have grown anywhere else.

I was thirteen years old when I saw the kung-fu film *The Thirty-sixth Chamber of Shaolin*, the story of a man who trains to be a Shaolin monk then leaves the temple to teach the world their style of kung fu. Nine years later, I formed the Wu-Tang Clan—and we left Staten Island to teach the world our style of hip-hop. Eight years after that, I came to the original Shaolin, saw the real Wu-Tang Mountain—and saw that it was all part of one whole. I saw that we really were what we'd always claimed to be: men of Wu-Tang.

Shaolin is about as far from Staten Island as you can get. It's on Mount Song, the center peak of Taoism's Five Great Mountains in China, a sacred place, high above the banks of the Yellow River. There on the mountain's western edge stands the Shaolin temple: low and sturdy, red walls and round windows, the same courtyard where monks have practiced kung fu ever since Da'Mo visited in the sixth century.

Shaolin is seven thousand miles from New York City. Wu-Tang Mountain is even farther. Five thousand feet above sea level, a five-hour bus ride through winding mountain roads, and a home to Taoist monasteries going back fifteen hundred years. But when we stood on this mountain and looked up at the range of peaks called the Nine Dragons, this is what we saw: three mountains forming a giant *W*—the symbol I chose to represent a crew of nine men, nine years earlier. It was as plain as day, and has been for a million years. But some things aren't visible until you're truly ready to see them.

I stood there with Shi Yan Ming, a man I call Sifu, which means "teacher." He's a thirty-fourth-generation Shaolin monk who defected to the United States the same year we formed Wu-Tang. As we looked over the mountains, Sifu and I talked about the original Wu-Tang—how it was founded by a monk named Zhang Sanfeng, who had been banished to this mountain for causing violence and doing wrong. Zhang Sanfeng came to the mountain to meditate and find God and eventually founded the Wu-Tang. Our crew had lots of meanings for the words *Wu-Tang*—"Witty, Unpredictable Talent and Natural Game," "We Usually Take Another Nigga's Garments"—in China, I learned another, the original one: "Man who is deserving of God."

So in that sense, we are all Wu-Tang. You are Wu-Tang. If you ever stood on a mountain or by an ocean and felt a deep connection, a vast infinite presence inside you, you felt it: what Taoists call Oneness, Muslims call Allah, others call God. That's what I felt on Wu-Tang Mountain, but it's also what I felt in Staten Island and even Dumont Avenue in Brooklyn—only dimmer, quieter. Allah's truth is within us all, all the time—a seed waiting for light to help it grow. Wisdom is the Light.

This is a book of Wisdom—an accumulation of songs, parables, meditations, and experiences to help manifest that truth in your life. Wisdom is what shows those in darkness the Light, what reveals the path or the Way. It's what we all need to live. The sutras of the Buddha teach that without wisdom there is no gain. In the Bible's Book of Proverbs, King Solomon chooses wisdom over all the other gifts that God offers him—long life, riches, fame—but through wisdom achieved these gifts and many more, including seven hundred wives. In Islam's Divine Mathematics, we learn that Wisdom is the Two after One, which is Knowledge—it is proof of knowledge, reflection of knowledge, knowledge in action. In my life, all these understandings of wisdom have proven true.

Krishna said that you can study all day, pray all day, chant all day, but you'll get to Heaven faster if you hang with wise men. I've been blessed by wise men my whole life—whether it was my cousin GZA, who first taught me Mathematics, my Chinese brother Sifu, who teaches me kung fu, or the philosophy students I met in Athens, the villagers I shared mud huts with in Africa, the audio inventors I worked with in Switzerland, the film directors in Hollywood, the mullahs of Egypt. The kind of artist that I am, I tend to meet people who want to show me something, and I'm always down to learn. In the Wu-Tang Clan, I'm known as the Abbot—which, like Sifu, means "teacher"—but a real teacher is also a student, someone who never stops learning.

The Book of Proverbs says that King Solomon sought wisdom from the cradle to the grave. That's a way of saying he sought rebirth. Just as you must come through a woman's womb to attain physical birth, so must you come through Wisdom to achieve mental birth. And like childbirth, Wisdom often comes with pain. Pain, joy, fear—all have borne in me wisdom, which, like water, is an ever flowing spring from a bottomless ocean, a flow of life that takes the shape of any vessel, that reveals itself in all bodies and all moments. For Wisdom is the Way.

You've been given the chance to hear the true and
    living
So do the knowledge, son, before you do the wisdom.

—RZA, "A Day to God Is 1,000 Years"

THE

TAO

OF

WU

THE CALL

From the heart of Medina
to the head of Fort Greene
Now-Y-C: Now I See Everything

—RZA, "N.Y.C. Everything"

Let the caller and the called disappear;
be lost in the call.

—Rumi

In every story and life, there's a call. In the Book of Exodus, it comes to Moses after he leaves Egypt as a shepherd: One of his sheep gets away, he goes looking for it on a mountain, and he hears a voice—God calling to him. In the Koran, it comes to Muhammad after he's had kids and has lived a full, righteous life: He's forty years old and meditating in a cave, and he hears a voice—

Allah calling him to be a prophet. Or look at San Te, in the film *Thirty-sixth Chamber*: He's out in the country-side rebelling against the Manchu government and sees a dude break a box of fish open with his bare hands. He asks him, "How'd you do that?' and the guy says, "It's kung fu; I learned it at Shaolin." That one word, *Shaolin*, was a call to San Te—what sent him to seek knowledge, become a monk, and spread the wisdom of kung fu around the world.

I believe the call can come to anyone, at any time. I know because it came to me, one night in a Staten Island housing project, in July of 1976.

I was born Robert Fitzgerald Diggs, in Brownsville, Brooklyn, to one of the biggest families in New York. My mother had eleven kids, so she's responsible for thirty-five, forty people. My great-uncle had eight children— one of whom would become Ol' Dirty Bastard—so that sprouted another forty, fifty people, and it goes on from there. Through marriage and bloodline, we spread across all five boroughs. Part of the reason is we were scattered from the beginning.

My family broke up when I was three years old. In my last memory of my father, he's holding me in one hand and a hammer in the other, smashing up the furniture. Since my mother couldn't afford to raise the five of us herself, she sent us away, and I went off to live with her father's family in North Carolina. That's where I got to know my uncle Hollis, the first wise man in my life.

Hollis had that Solomon kind of wisdom. He was a doctor, a wealthy man with hundreds of acres of land, many adopted children, and a joy of life that followed him everywhere. He was the kind of man you'd have to call enlightened. Every one of my mom's brothers and sisters had a different father, and her father's family didn't like my grandmother, who had my moms when she was sixteen. But Hollis had love for his brother's daughter. He was always checking up on her, trying to put her in school—although she never went, and just kept having kids instead. But Hollis had a compulsion to take care of these kids, especially me.

As soon as I got down to North Carolina, Hollis started teaching me things, setting aside books for me to read, saying, "Bobby, I want you to study." Before I turned four, I was doing my older brother's homework. From Hollis I learned about science and religion, but also poetry and spoken word. One of the first books he gave me was a collection of Mother Goose rhymes—which I started memorizing immediately—and he was always going around saying these strange verses.

"Never cry when a hearse goes by," he'd say. "Because you may be the next to die. They'll cover you with a cold white sheet. They'll put you down about six feet deep. It's not so bad the first few weeks, until you start to mumble and creep, and the worms crawl in and the worms crawl out, and the ants play pinochle on your snout, your stomach turns the sickest green as pus runs out like thick whipped cream . . ." It was an old Southern folk rhyme—one of many Hollis used to say—and before long I started saying it myself.

Hollis also took us to church every Sunday. It was an old Southern Baptist church where the services bugged me out. I loved the Bible stories I was reading, but I didn't like this room where people were falling out, catching the Holy Ghost, slobbering all over the place. That happened in a lot of black churches, and I could immediately see it was phony. The screaming and moaning just didn't *feel* right. The spirit of God sounded beautiful to me, but I quickly separated the experience of God from church. I just couldn't see God in the fake-ass preachers or people wallowing on the ground. But I could see him in Hollis, my first real teacher.

Then, when I was seven, my mother called us back to New York. Eight of us moved in with her at Marcus Garvey projects in Brooklyn. There, a different kind of education began.

Our place was on Dumont Avenue, right across the street from Betsy Head Pool—a vicious, violent place, the kind you definitely weren't coming back from with your sneakers. Kids from Brownsville projects, Tilden projects, Van Dyke projects, and Marcus Garvey used to hang out there, and two guys named Bighead Mike hung at the basketball court next door. One was Mike Tyson, the other was a drug dealer who later shot up our stoop trying to get a rival dealer (who happened to be my friend Chili Wop).

My second night living there, I got jacked at the store by three teenagers. When I got home, my mother asked me what happened. When I told her, she grabbed me and a butcher's knife and, still in her nightgown, walked me back to the store, looking for these motherfuckers. That was when I got a sense of the family with me now.

But the fact is, at this point I was a nerd: deep into books, saying "Yes, sir, no, ma'am," going to church every Sunday. I may have been staying in the hood, but I was living in my head. That changed in the summer of 1976.

Something was happening in New York that year. There was a force in the air that didn't have a name yet. And this one afternoon, it was alive at a block party in the Park Hill projects in Staten Island. I had come by to visit my cousin Gary, who would become the GZA. There, between the two buildings where kids played stickball, some DJs had plugged their systems into the lights. I remember walking in, hearing the sound, feeling the energy, and getting sucked in.

It was DJ Jones, and the MCs were MC Punch and Quincy. They were on the mike saying just a couple of very simple rhymes, the same two or three lines all night long. That was rap way back then—just one or two phrases repeated. Like a mantra. And when I heard that beat and those rhymes, I felt a euphoria I can't even explain. I ended up staying there through the night, not getting back to the house until eleven o'clock and getting an ass-whupping from my mother.

Because in that parking lot, I heard the love of my life calling to me.

The night was cooling off; I was dancing with a girl—me just eight years old and doing the wop, grinding up on her, freaking her. Then I heard one of those MCs.

Back then, songs were sung. Instruments were played. This was the voice of a man speaking words over music. It sounds crazy now—I've written thousands and thousands of lyrics since then, even lyrics jumping off Hollis's folk rhymes with the group Gravediggaz, on an album called *Six Feet Deep*. But that night, these were the first words I heard spoken over a beat. It's like it says in the Gospel of John: "In the beginning was the Word." And to me, those words weren't just rap lyrics. They spoke to something inherent in me. If you ask my older brother, he'll tell you I was reading Dr. Seuss in rhyme and rhythm at age three. But up until that night, I'd been living in my head. These words and this music, they were a call—a call to something deep inside me. They were a call to my soul. And it came in a simple party rap, a few lines that went on through the night.

Dip-dip, dive
So-so-cialize
Clean out your ears
Open your eyes

Open your mind, body, and soul

to God's voice in whatever

vessel that bears it. Let it pull

you into the world.

ISLAND

A PARABLE OF SOLITUDE

I spent my formative years on an island—Staten Island—which is a blessing I've taken with me through life. Many cultures consider an island to be the ideal home. First, because you're surrounded by water, which is life. Second, because you're isolated from the masses, which allows you to find yourself, to develop inner strengths you couldn't find anywhere else. An island shows you the true nature of life itself.

In Staten Island, Wu-Tang niggas were set apart from all the influences and fads that were happening in the other four boroughs. I believe that while everything else in hip-hop culture was in constant flux, this island was nurturing something ancient. When you watch a movie like *Godzilla*, you see them go out to one of these tiny remote islands and find Mothra. It was the same way with us. A nine-man hip-hop crew based on Mathematics, chess, comics, and kung-fu flicks wasn't springing up in the middle of a Manhattan art scene. Only on a remote island can something like King Kong grow to his full capacity.

When I first bought a house out in New Jersey, I got it as a Wu house, but the rest of the members couldn't stand being there—they wanted to be in the city. But for me this remote house, this island, was the best place to be. It's a place to break off the antennas on top of buildings, to break away from those frequencies, to break away from everybody's hustle and negativity. A place to reconnect with your own strength.

My kung-fu teacher Sifu would come out to this house to train me. My uncle, who was also a martial artist, used to live and train there too. In fact, it was out in this island that he developed a style he called the Universal African Fighting Style. Eventually, he ended up being inducted into the Martial Arts Hall of Fame, all because he had developed something special—a combination of jujitsu, karate, and samurai.

My uncle was inducted by Moses Powell, the jujitsu expert who founded the style known as Sanuces Ryu. Powell passed away recently, but he was one of the top black martial artists in the country. He trained CIA men, demonstrated for the United Nations, and taught warriors in many different fields. But when my uncle went to study with him, he told my uncle something important. He said, "What *you* got is unique." He let him know that he was blessed, that he had it already within him.

I advise everyone to find an island in this life. Find a

place where this culture can't take energy from you, sap your will and originality. Since anything physical can be mental, that island can be your home. Turn off the electromagnetic waves being forced upon you, the countless invisible forces coming at you all the time.

Find an island;

turn inward;

discover your

true strength.

THE ART OF LISTENING

A man thinks seven times before he speaks. It's harder to make the glass than break the glass.

On the corner of my block there stood this old man
A black immigrant from the land of Sudan
Who used to tell stories to the children in the building
But never had a dollar to keep his pocket filled in
He bombed, he knew Deuteronomy the science of astronomy
But didn't know the basic principles of economy
I say the wise man don't play the role of a fool
The first thing a man must obtain is Twelve Jewelz
Knowledge Wisdom Understanding to help you achieve
Freedom, Justice, Equality, Food, Clothing, and Shelter
After this, Love, Peace, and Happiness
He had the nappiest head, I told him total satisfaction
Is to achieve one goal in the scheme of things
He who works like a slave, eats like a king

—"TWELVE JEWELZ," GRAVEDIGGAZ

When I stayed down South, Uncle Hollis was my teacher. In the streets of New York, we taught each other. Cousins, hustlers, gangsters—they were all part of my extended family, and each one taught me something. For example, when I was nine my cousin Vince turned me on to kung-fu flicks. He'd take me to the Forty-second Street theaters in Manhattan, where they played triple features for $1.50. That's where I first saw the Shaw Brothers' *The Five Deadly Venoms*, a film that sparked a lifelong obsession. By the time *The Empire Strikes Back* came out, in 1979, everyone at school was talking about that. I'd be saying, "You seen *Five Deadly Venoms*?" and no one knew what I was talking about.

But in 1980, another cousin hooked me up with some different wisdom, a kind they weren't talking about in school. And for me, this wisdom changed the whole world.

All through 1978 and '79, as I was living in Brownsville—writing rhymes, chasing hip-hop, digging kung-fu flicks—I kept looking forward to trips down South. I was hoping to get more one-on-one time with Uncle Hollis, to learn from this man who was like a father to me. Then after about a year of life in Brooklyn, my great-grandfather came over to bring me the news: Uncle Hollis passed away from a heart attack.

That was the probably the last time I cried until my moms died, decades later. I mean, like, *cry, cry, cry*, like how they cry in the Bible—wailing, gnashing teeth. It was the most painful experience of my life, and it secured my poverty. When Hollis passed there was no more connection to that family. Now my mother was four months behind in the rent, landlords were telling us to get out. We were about to lose our home—to go from next-to-nothing to nothing.

But right around that time, my cousin Daddy-O asked me something. He said, "Yo, you heard about those Twelve Jewels?"

I didn't know what he meant. Daddy-O was a street hustler, a cool guy, not a spiritual man. But it turned out he was also a Muslim, someone whose other name, his righteous name, was Born Knowledge. He explained that these weren't physical jewels, like someone in the hood wore to display his wealth. They were mental jewels—principles, ways of life—and that by obtaining them you would find a different kind of wealth. He said the Jewels were part of something called "the Lessons"—teachings from the Nation of Islam.

It would be a year or two before I heard about the Lessons or the Nation again. In fact, you're not even supposed to learn the Twelve Jewels first, you're supposed to learn them third—after the Supreme Mathematics and the Supreme Alphabet. But back then all I wanted to know about were those Jewels. And even today, the Jewels are the precepts I advocate most.

The Jewels are as follows: Knowledge, Wisdom, Understanding, Freedom, Justice, Equality, Food, Clothing, Shelter, Love, Peace, and Happiness. Each jewel has its own profound meaning, and each one takes work and meditation to achieve, but they break down like a chain reaction.

First a man gets Knowledge, which is knowledge of self. Then he gets Wisdom, which is the reflection of that knowledge. Then he gets Understanding, which is the power to act on Wisdom. With Understanding he sees that he has Freedom—that he has *freed* his *dome* from ignorance—which means he has free will. But Freedom operates under a law: the law of Justice. That means that I'm free to smack you in your face, but justice applies: There will be a reward or penalty for my actions. Therefore, I must deal with Equality, because all men are created equal. By showing Equality to one another we're activating Freedom, Justice, and Equality—the fourth-through-sixth jewels.

Now, those are all things that build a man's character. And after you attain them, you're able to strive for Food, Clothing, and Shelter—which also have both physical and mental meanings. Obviously, food is nourishment, shelter is a home, and clothing is protection. But *mental* food is food from the tree of life—wisdom, science, history, food for your mind. *Mental* clothing is how you carry yourself—the way you walk, the way you move and speak. If you have clothed yourself in righteousness, even the bummiest clothing has dignity. And *mental* shelter is the mind's protection from the evil atmosphere—the lies and corruption of the outside world. So if you have these three jewels, your home is like a king's even if you're living in a shack.

Soon enough, that's exactly how I was living. Right after Daddy-O told me about the Jewels, my family was kicked out of our home. My two brothers and I wound up in with our grandparents on 64 Targee Street in Staten Island. There the only mathematics being practiced was addition. First we were five. Then my aunt and her husband came back from the army and moved in with their daughter. We were eight. A month later, my uncle, his wife, and his daughter moved in from Minnesota. We were eleven. Then my other uncle, who was gay, popped up with his friend—another gay dude who dressed like a woman—and *they* moved in. We were thirteen. This kept up until I counted nineteen people living in a two-bedroom. Your bed was whatever spot you could grab on the floor. Your blankets were those gray wool mats that movers use to protect furniture.

That's poverty in this country—something that makes you small, shrinks your horizon, clouds your vision. But even when I was living like that, because of what Daddy-O told me, I had faith that my mind could transform my

surroundings. Mathematics would form my first governing principles, but the Jewels had the biggest impact on
me. And that's probably because of when they found
me—right when everything else was being taken away.

With the idea of the Jewels, I got a sense that even if
my body was in hell, my mind wasn't. Most people let
their body lead their mind. When someone has a drug
addiction, his body is addicted to the drug. Heroin is a
physical addiction: If you don't get it, you get sick. But
even though your body is addicted, your mind chastises
you every time you use it. When your mind has attained
these Jewels, it leads the body. So even if you're in a physical hell, by seeking the Twelve Jewels you let your mind
lead your body to Heaven.

You don't get all Twelve Jewels at once—you have to
strive for them, prepare yourself for them. But after you
attain the first nine, then you're ready to make your life
truly satisfying. That's when you can attain Love, which is
the highest elevation of Understanding—either between
two people or between all members of mankind. And after
you attain Love, then you have Peace, and finally you get
Happiness—which is total and complete satisfaction with
yourself. This means you realize that nothing and nobody
else can make you happy. Happiness is something you get
from yourself. If you're completely satisfied with yourself,
nobody can take it away from you.

Years later, I realized that this principle, the last of the
Twelve Jewels, applies to everyone, everywhere in the

world. Two decades after my time on Targee Street, I went to West Africa—as a rich and famous man. I went to visit my cousin and Wu-Tang brother Ghostface, who had gone to get treated for diabetes by a bush doctor that his herbalist in Staten Island recommended. The doctor's village was deep in the country of Benin—hours from any city, a place with no running water, where people lived in mud huts and slept on the floor. At this point, I'd lived in the Trump Plaza, in a million-dollar home; I'd been hanging with millionaires and even billionaires. I came to Benin having just stayed at the Metropolitan Hotel in London, at the Grand Hyatt in France, and in the London home of Richard Branson, the mogul who founded Virgin. I came to West Africa from the height of wealth and was blessed with a new understanding of poverty.

The first place you reach from the airport is Cotonou, a crowded city of about a million people. Everyone there lives in apartment buildings and strives for a Western lifestyle. But when Ghost came in to meet me there, he'd been in the village awhile. He was wearing an African dashiki, his hair had grown out, and he had a full beard: He looked like an African villager. Everybody on the street was dismissive of Ghost. But everyone was being cool with me—trying to shake my hand and be my friend—because I was dressed in hip-hop clothes. They thought I was somebody and Ghost was nobody. They were trying to be like Americans.

I got into this beat-up Peugeot with Ghost and the

bush doctor's right-hand man, and we headed out to the village. When we got there, I noticed something else. In the city, just about everyone I met had his hand out— either asking for something or trying to sell me something. When we got to the village, everyone had his hand out in offering—either something to eat, or directions, or some kind of help. They had less but they were offering more.

I had brought some kung-fu flicks with me because Ghost was jonesing and the bush doctor was into kung fu. So we sat in a hut before the one TV in the village and watched *Blade of Fury*—a great movie, about a revolution where all the revolutionaries get killed but one kid survives and the master is still happy because he realizes that the revolution will be carried on. As we watched, all the kids in the village stood outside and watched through the window while we, the honored guests, sat inside.

Years before, when we were living in the Park Hill projects in Staten Island, we'd always wonder why the Africans moving in seemed so happy. They were crammed into a room just like us but they were happy. They *liked* the projects. We hated the projects. The projects are the worst place you can be if you're watching TV, reading magazines, seeing people who have jobs and live in houses. We didn't understand the gangbangers in California. I'd always complain, "They flippin' this set and that set and these motherfuckers got *houses*! We've got to live where you got two niggas on top of you, two niggas beside you, and neighbors that you hear moving around you at all times!"

But in Africa, I saw these people living on dirt. They had nothing but food, clothing, and shelter—and a love of themselves. And so they had happiness, the Twelfth Jewel. It's within all of us. Western culture just makes it harder to find.

Of course, back when I was a kid, I wasn't looking too hard.

A year after Hollis died and Daddy-O told me about the Twelve Jewels, I had settled into life in the hood. Mad changes happen at that age, and by 1980 I was a street kid, a hip-hop fiend. I hated school and waited for each weekend, when I'd hang out with my cousin Gary, who would become the GZA, or my other cousin Russell, who would become Ol' Dirty Bastard. Sugar Hill Gang's "Rapper's Delight" came out the year before and showed us you could make a record with rhymes, so I wrote at least twenty songs that year, setting them to my mom's R&B records.

Gary was a couple of years older and the guy who introduced me to hip-hop, so naturally I looked up to him. And one spring day, that respect opened a door to enlightenment. You could say hip-hop was the vessel, but the message was Allah.

At the time, I was staying at 64 Targee Street, right by the Stapleton projects. Gary lived at 55 Bowing Street, in the Park Hill projects—one of the toughest in New

York. To get there I could either walk a straight line down the street outside the projects, or I could go to the store, through Stapleton, and then through Park Hill. For some reason, I was the kind of kid who'd walk through two projects to get where I was going.

I'd go to the store first—a little corner Puerto Rican bodega—and I'd ask the hot dog guy, Mr. Harry, for food. I'd say, "Mr. Harry, I don't got no money, can I have a donut?" And he'd give me a donut, maybe give me a hot dog. Then, I'd head into the projects.

Everything was there: the music, the people, the sound, the color—the place was alive. They had block parties going on all the time then—DJ Jones, Dr. Rock and the Force M.D.s—all playing in the park or on the plaza. So this one beautiful day in May, I came into those projects for hip-hop—to hear the music in the street and write rhymes with Gary. But I went home with something even deeper.

The minute I showed up, something about Gary was different. For one thing, he had a different name. We always used to call him by his government name, Gary, his nickname, Buck, or his rapper name, Gangsta G. But this day he said, "My name is Allah Justice." Then he told me about Knowledge: the first chamber of study in the Nation of Gods and Earths.

He said, "Yo, Knowledge is the basic foundation of all life." And I was like, "Whatchu mean?" We were standing outside his building, a block away from where I heard that first hip-hop party four years earlier. But for some reason, what GZA started saying and the way he said it hit me even harder than the MCs I'd heard that night.

He told me about Mathematics and Knowledge of Self and God. "He's not a spirit," GZA said. "God is you; he's inside you." Then he showed me a white sheet of paper. On the top were bold letters that read, "All Praise Is Due to Allah, Lord of All the World." It was the first page from the Divine Lessons, from the Nation of Gods and Earths.

The Gods were the next generation of the Nation of Islam, whose teachings had shaped giants like Malcolm X and Muhammad Ali. The newer school was founded in 1964, by a Harlem student minister known as Clarence 13X, who we now call the Father. He was looking for a quicker and more powerful way to bring those teachings directly to America's black youth, so he condensed the Nation's Lost-Found Lessons into a philosophical core called the 120, which formed the basis of the Lessons taught by the Five Percent Nation in New York—lessons that had transformed my cousin Gary into Allah Justice.

After we finished talking, Allah Justice gave me that first page of Lessons to read on my own. At this point, I was miles from Uncle Hollis and his books. No one else I respected was telling me to get an education, but GZA did. He told me to educate myself, to seek knowledge on my own. We talked for a bit more, then I headed home in a kind of trance.

All the way home, about a mile-long walk, I kept hearing in my mind, "God, God, God." I walked past a fish and chips place with a pinball machine ringing inside. "God, God, God . . ." I walked past a Chinese restaurant, past a pizzeria. "God, God, God . . ." I walked down Targee by the Stapleton projects, which loomed like the Death Star. "God, God, God. . . ." Then I passed a Christian church.

In the streets, spiritual messages come in pamphlets. As I went by this church, a dude out front handed me one. It said "The Bread of Life." I took it and kept walking.

When I got home I memorized that sheet of Mathematics quickly, but I was still hungry for Knowledge. So I memorized the Christian pamphlet's teaching about the Gospel of John. I'd heard Bible stories my whole life, but now that I had this personalized idea of Knowledge in my head, it made the lessons of the Bible seem stronger. This time I understood how to read the Bible, how to look at it for what's real in my heart instead of what somebody's telling me. That night, I started reading the Bible. And kept reading until I finished it.

The ancient Chinese philosopher Meng-tzu wrote, "Truth out of season bears no fruit." To me, that means two things. One: There's a time and place for every kind of knowledge to flourish. Two: The personal characteristics of great messengers are usually irrelevant. For instance, they say that Martin Luther King Jr. was a fornicator. Does it matter? Do you believe in the messenger or his message? I believe in the message. That's why when I read certain books or see certain films, I skip over the names: Forget who said it if it's truth. For some reason, I've always felt that way, that knowledge is like God, out there behind labels and images. Eastern thought, Christianity, comic books, kung fu: They all have truths, and each truth has a season—either in history or in your own life. And in the spring season of 1980, I was blessed with the truth of Divine Mathematics, through my cousin and enlightener, GZA.

The next day, after I stayed up all night reading the Bible, I went back to him and started quoting back to him what I learned from the pamphlet and that first set of Lessons. He was impressed with that, and he gave me the next set. It was time for me to find Knowledge, but that meant that first I had to find Knowledge of Self.

This is one kind of knowledge you can't seek. It's something you have to let happen to you—through meditation, sitting quiet and alone, in contemplation. In the early '80s, when you came to Mathematics, you had to fast for three days before they gave you the Knowledge and began your training. It was like the test they give a Shaolin novice, to see if he's centered and committed. I did it when I was eleven.

After I officially began my studies of the Lessons, GZA gave me the rest of the Divine Mathematics and the Divine Alphabet. Then I had to choose a name. He told me to think of my own name. I thought for a long time and came up with Rakeem. He approved because he could call me "Ra" and my moms would think he was saying "Rob."

This was important—parents were kicking kids out for taking names, getting Lessons.

The Five Percent had a reputation as a gang, as vicious, terrifying criminals. Even when I first heard GZA talking about the Five Percent, my first thought was, *Hold on, ain't those the guys that beat up my uncle last year?* The rep came because a lot of them were tough niggas from jail who never really let those ways go, who weren't living the Lessons righteously—or were doing it imperfectly, let's say. They hadn't let go of their negative side. Turns out, neither had I.

I started studying the Lessons with my brother, Universal King. I loved the shit out of King, but he was a bully big brother. Today I realize that he made us all into warriors, but he did so much violence to us growing up that I didn't like him. So it was good to have something to build love between us, but it only went so far. At a certain point, my frustration with him came between me and righteousness. One day, we had a fight and I lost, as usual, and after this fight, I told him, "Fuck you! I ain't righteous no more!" And I ate a pork chop on him—smothered in gravy, on a bed of rice. I figured that was the only way to hurt him. When I did that, I stopped reading the Lessons. I stopped believing out of anger.

But a year or so later, I was sitting down at the table at my grandmother's house, and my aunt's boyfriend was over. He was a heroin addict and clearly fucked up: nappy head, scraggly beard—he looked kind of like a wino Jesus—and he kept nodding off. My grandmother was making some food and asked him, "You want some hot dogs, Donald?" And he said, "There better not be any pork in it." When I heard him say that—just mumbling in a kind of daze—it spoke to me. Then he looked at me and said, "The Lessons are right; the Gods are right." When he finished talking he got up and left, and my heart opened again.

In a way, this doped-up, nappy-headed junkie was like an angel. He wasn't living the Lessons anymore and it showed. What my heart heard from him was, "Those lessons will save your life." I was twelve years old. That night got me back into it.

The point is, sometimes you have to be called more than once. The angel called the Prophet Muhammad saying, "Read." Muhammad was illiterate and said, "I can't read." *"Read,"* the angel said again. "I can't read," Muhammad said. Then the angel said: *"In the name of Allah who created man from a drop of blood—READ."* And it was the third time that he felt it.

My first call came from Daddy-O telling me about the Twelve Jewels. I heard it but didn't follow. The second came from GZA, who enlightened me, started me on the path, but I drifted out of anger. The third came from a dope fiend, a man who once had Knowledge of Self but lost it, fell away into darkness. His call was the same as the other ones, but he was a living example of what happens when you stray.

After that, I dove back into the lessons, mastered them in seven months. I didn't tell anybody. I fasted by myself. I studied only in the bathroom. And when I finally got up to the 1-to-14, the level my brother was at, a level good enough to be a man with it and really understand it, I told him. We were brothers again—but in a deeper way than before. The third call was my final call. I was convinced. And once I mastered these lessons, I was able to understand every step of my life.

The Lessons begin with the 120. That's 120 lessons or degrees that help you understand man's relationship to the universe. I learned the 120 faster than anyone else in my neighborhood and had them down by the time I was twelve years old. But it was only later that I realized just how deep they really were, how the wisdom of Mathematics connected to the jewels of Eastern, Western, scientific, and religious thought—and to the knowledge I already had in my heart. That's because Mathematics is also what Euclid said it is: a description of the thoughts of God. And the only way to get to God is to find him within yourself.

But in Mathematics, the method of instruction has a

power of its own. When the Father brought these lessons to lost and confused young black men like me, he was promising a transformation that the lessons actually provide. That fact is, if you get through the rigors of study with the Gods, you truly are a different person.

The 120 breaks down to 120 questions and answers. The first few, called the 1-to-10, are ten questions that begin with "Who is the original man?" The answer is: "The original man is the Asiatic Black man, the Maker, the Owner, the Cream of the planet Earth, the Father of Civilization, and God of the Universe." You have to memorize each question and answer verbatim, with every single article, noun, and verb correct. After the 1-to-10 comes the 1-to-36—which are thirty-six phrases. When I was learning them, I'd say, "My name is Prince Rakeem, I came to North America by myself. My uncle was brought over here by a trader three hundred and seventy-nine years ago. My uncle does not know he's my uncle. He doesn't speak his own language." The phrases go on and on.

After mastering these, you move on to the 1-to-14, which are more intense. By this time, the answers are pages long. If you get through them, you've memorized thousands and thousands of words, in precise order. The main lesson people tend to get stuck on is the Fourth, or Culture, Degree, from the 1-to-14. That's the one that deals with a man named Yacub, whose biblical name would be Jacob, father of the white race. What hangs students up here isn't the idea that the white race was a diabolical experiment—any poor, black kid feels that way at some point in his life—it's the length of the question and precision of the phrasing. The question reads: "Why do we run Yacub and his made Devil from the roots of civilization over the hot Arabian desert into the caves of West Asia as they now called Europe? What is the meaning of E.U. and Rope? How long ago was it? What did the Devil bring with him? What kind of life did the Devil live then? How long was it before Musa came to teach the Devil their forgotten trick knowledge?" That's just the question. Now just imagine how long the answer is. The Born Degree, which comes after, is even longer.

To a lot of guys in the ghetto, this was their education. I knew brothers who only graduated fifth grade yet were scientists because of the Lessons. They learned geology, geometry, astronomy, physics, history—all of it came through the Lessons. What is the circumference of the Earth? "The circumference of the planet Earth is approximately 25,000 miles." What is the diameter of the Earth? "The diameter of the Earth is 7,926 miles." The total square miles of the Earth—total square miles of land, total square miles of water. The weight of the planet. The speed of light, the speed of sound. You learned more than you would in school.

The Lessons are a map to realization—they lead you to it in steps. The first step, or degree, is Knowledge. We refer to the first task in any situation as "doing the knowledge," which means to look, listen, and observe. But the power of the Lessons didn't just come from the information they provided; it also came from their actual vocabulary and the cadence. It's like how they say that the Koran can be truly understood only in Arabic, because of the cadence of the language. The act of internalizing these Lessons transforms you; it strengthens your mind.

A few years ago, some British researchers did a study on cab drivers in London. They scanned their brains and found that the ones who had the most time on the streets had the largest hippocampi—which is the part of the brain that handles memory. By mastering the streets in that city, they actually increased the size and changed the structure of their brains. In order to get qualified, each cab driver had to go through a training period in which they mastered all the geography in the city. What do they call this? Doing the knowledge.

See, I believe the Lessons provide something that everyone, of any race, needs: a sense of perspective—of the size of the world, the scale of the universe, the place of man. The Earth has only 57,250,000 square miles of land on it. And out of that, only 29 million is useful. This kind of information grounds you, shrinks your problems and expands your horizons at the same time. You can hear its wisdom in a verse by one of the greatest rappers of all time, Rakim: "What would you say as the Earth gets further and further away / Planets as small as balls of clay / Stray into the Milky Way, world's out of sight / As far as the eye can see, not even a satellite." That's a mind transformed by the Lessons.

Mathematics contains universal truths, but no one needed its wisdom more than poor black men at the end of the last century. So many of us were so lost—deprived of knowledge of self, of others, of the world we lived in. Even in the Islamic world, commentaries on Muslim books were teaching that the black man comes from the grandson of Noah, who was Ham—a man who was cursed, made to be despised, a servant, a slave. That's a myth, but it was a myth taught in both mosques and Christian churches, a myth taught to the slaves as well.

If you were poor and black, Mathematics attacked the idea that you were meant to be ignorant, uneducated, blind to the world around you. It exposed the lies that helped people treat your forefathers as animals. And it wasn't until someone like the Father came to actively disseminate this information to poor black men—saying, "Hold on, your people are the fathers of civilization"— that people like me were set free. I can now say that if it wasn't for Mathematics, I wouldn't have achieved anything. I never would have imagined that a poor black motherfucker like me would grow up to respect the world, his fellow man, or himself.

The same thing happened to Malcolm X—he's in jail,

going through hell, and a man comes and tells him, "You ain't no nigger. You're from the tribe of Shabbaz." And right then, all his self-hatred turned to ashes. He heard the call and from every day on he was alive.

That's what the Lessons did for me. They gave me guidance, understanding, and freedom.

But freedom from yourself? That's often a whole different story.

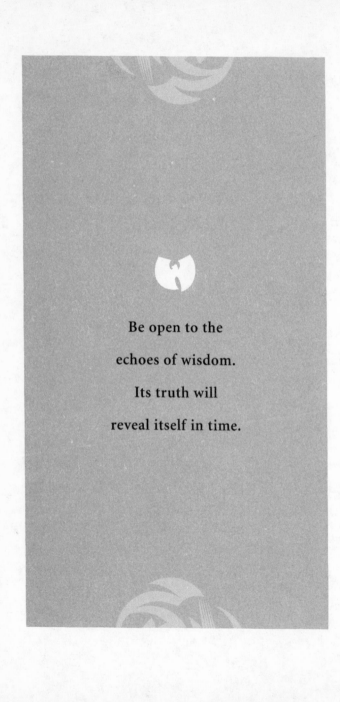

Be open to the

echoes of wisdom.

Its truth will

reveal itself in time.

FEAR

I was afraid as a child. I was afraid of everything. I was scared of water—I couldn't swim—I was scared of trucks on the turnpike, and mostly I was scared of ghosts. But at some point, I realized something. A ghost is something you create yourself—a man's mind makes it happen. If there were nobody on Earth, would a ghost still have a chance to spook somebody? No. You manifest ghosts through fear.

The words of Marcus Garvey resonated with me. He said, "Fear is a state of nervousness only fit for children. Men should not fear. The only thing man should fear is God. To fear anything other than God is to offend God." I carry that to this day: Enlightened men do not fear.

HORROR

They say wisdom is the wise words spoken
by a brother attempting to open
the graves of these mentally dead slaves

—RZA, "The Birth (Broken Hearts)"

In this culture, some of the deepest wisdom comes from horror movies. A perfect example is *Night of the Living Dead*. That movie and its sequels teach you about life.

For one thing, *Night of the Living Dead* predicted the dawn of crack. If you lived in the hood in the '80s, you saw that movie come to life on the street. There's a reason Public Enemy titled that song "Night of the Living Baseheads."

Secondly, *Dawn of the Dead* was the great metaphor for American society. The zombies were Americans, just walking through the mall, lost, trying to find excitement outside of themselves. They forgot that excitement is not buying a new TV; it's taking your shoes off and walking in the grass in your backyard. All those movies were really showing us ourselves.

When I first saw *Night of the Living Dead*, I was scared to death. But when I watched it again at age sixteen (when they were up to *Day of the Dead*), I'd gotten knowledge of myself, and could relate to what it was saying about America. The dead were alive, but they were blind, deaf, and dumb. So to me, they were symbolic of black men in America.

The dead in those movies are alive—that's just a description of physical matter, it's active—but they don't have life. Life comes when you have knowledge, wisdom, and understanding, when you can see for real, touch and feel for real, know for real. Then you are truly living.

Finally, all the *Of the Dead* films work as metaphors for the Five Percent. The survivors are holdouts living among the mentally dead. And interestingly, they tend to be led by black men. At the same time, though, after the black man survives—he fights off destruction through the whole movie—a white man kills him.

CHESS LESSONS

When I was eleven years old, three major changes hit me: 1) I found Knowledge of Self; 2) I lost my virginity; 3) I learned to play chess. The last two were actually with the same person—an older girl in the neighborhood—but then again we call women "wisdom," so maybe it was meant to be. Chess became a source of wisdom that has been with me my whole life.

The game began centuries ago in India. In a way, it's metaphysics as a board game. The board's number of squares is sixty-four, which is a crucial number in Mathematics. Sixty-four is also the number of creation. When the sperm meets the egg and they have meiosis, it splits into sixty-four separate cells—two to four, four to eight, then eight to sixty-four: the basic number of life. When people say "Chess is life," they may not even know how much truth they're speaking.

Chess is also a martial art. It's about combat and directing chi. When you're on a streak in chess, you're usually on a streak in everything in your life. You're in balance, you're pushing energy forth, you're an unbeatable warrior. I know that happens with me. If I'm on point in my life, you better not test me on the chessboard. You'll lose.

I used to play older men in Wall Street around the same time that Josh Waitzkin—the child chess prodigy who inspired the movie *Searching for Bobby Fischer*—was whupping older dudes' asses in Washington Square Park. I'm a fan of Bobby Fischer and a fan of Josh, who's now a friend. Years after he was the world chess champion for his age group, he went on to become a martial arts champ, and he says that chess revealed the learning ability that would allow him to dominate Tai Chi Chuan. Chess will do that. Even the simplest game teaches you something.

Probably the simplest game of all is the one called Fool's Mate. It's checkmate in four moves, but it takes no talent. If white moves first and goes to F4, black leaves his queen free with a move like E6—just moving his pawn once. His queen is then free to go to H5. If black goes to G3, white goes to H5 and there's no way to block an attack on the king. If you beat someone with this strategy, they're not a worthy opponent. If you win with this strategy, you played yourself.

But that works two ways. The most important thing is to realize that the problem is on the board, it's not with you. I ask people what piece they are on the chessboard. And some people say "I'm the king" or "I'm the knight." And then they ask me what piece I am, and I say, "I'm no piece. I take the position of God." Even if the king gets checkmated it doesn't stop me. It's the *king* that got check-mated, not me. You could call it a Zen approach to chess. And it also works in life.

I'm an American and I'm very patriotic when it comes to chess. I'd rather imitate Bobby Fischer than imitate Garry Kasparov. Fischer's way of thinking was more aggressive. They found out years later by using computers to analyze his games that he should have lost some of the games he won, but he was determined not to lose. Every time they had him in a so-called losing position, his will and determination would make him win. It was something besides pure mathematical insight, statistics, probability, and strategy. There was some spark in Fischer, his obsession to win, that helped him triumph.

I think most of my approach to life has been like that, to find order in chaos, to be in the middle of a bunch of things happening at the same time, but find focus. I strive to be like the sun sitting in the middle of the solar system with all the planets spinning around it—millions of things going on. It's just sitting there being the sun, but exerting gravitational effect on everything. I think man should look at himself that way. Similarly to the sun or to the nucleus of an atom, and all the confusing things going on around him are okay as long as he's staying focused on what he's doing as long as he's being himself.

Bobby Fischer lost when he became the pieces. When

he'd lose he'd go to his room and cry; he really took things hard. He couldn't separate what happened on the board from what happened to himself. And some people think that it drove him crazy. I don't think he was crazy. I think he was eccentric. But I think he lost a crucial part of perspective that you need in the game and in life.

In the end, the best strategy, the best tactic you can have in chess is the same one you should use in life: Never give up. Never let them count you out. That's how the greats play, right down to the last move. That's one more reason why chess is like a swordfight. It's to the death. You should play it that way, like you should live your life, as a game with mortal stakes. A game you play right down to the last move.

CHAMBERS

Knowing others is wisdom.
Knowing yourself is Enlightenment.

—LAO-TZU

I've been a story reader since I was three, a storyteller almost as long. When I was ten, I was friends with a Sudanese Muslim kid named Cassim, who knew a lot of the same Bible stories I did, since people like Job and Abraham are also mentioned in the Koran. The two of us would post up in the hood, telling tales of the prophets to other kids. That's what the Bible was to me back then—stories—until I found Knowledge, and the truth in them became real.

For years, it was the same way with kung-fu flicks. From the first time I saw *The Five Deadly Venoms*, in 1978,

I was hooked—hooked on the fighting, the period, the locales, and the stories. But the truth of those stories didn't hit me for a few years. Then, one day in 1983, when I was almost fourteen, I was watching TV. The screen flashed a commercial for next week's movie: "On June 6—*The Thirty-sixth Chamber of Shaolin*." That was some prophetic numerology—6, 6, 36—and the movie had just that kind of impact on me. It was like something from the Old Testament or a Greek epic. It changed my life, for real, because its wisdom brought my own story alive.

The Shaw Brothers made the movie in 1978, but it's about a man in the eighteenth century who becomes a Shaolin monk. The man, San Te, starts out as a college student learning ethics. When he hears about the revolution against the Manchus, who are oppressing the native people, he joins the revolution and becomes a messenger. He gets wounded in a Manchu attack and seeks refuge from the monks of the Shaolin temple. At first, they reject him because he's an ignorant outsider, but then the abbot there sees something in him. He begins training him in martial arts.

San Te starts out the film knowing nothing. By the end, he's a master. He completes all thirty-five chambers of Shaolin training faster than any other student—finishing them in seven years. Then he wants to start a thirty-sixth chamber to teach the wisdom of Shaolin to the world. I was fourteen years old when I saw that film. I had Knowledge of Self, had mastered the 120 faster than anyone my age, and was teaching Mathematics to others. When I saw *The Thirty-sixth Chamber*, I felt like I was living it.

The story is about oppression and transformation. The Manchus are oppressors; the students are the oppressed. But it takes the older monks to show them they're oppressed—they thought things were always like that. As a Mathematician, I could relate to that on a variety of levels—the students' blindness, the teachers' wisdom, the reality of the oppression, and the strength it would take to overcome it.

The second part of the movie is about the kung-fu training San Te goes through, and that *really* inspired me—started me doing push-ups, punching walls, going to Chinatown to buy kung-fu books. But it also confirmed the path I was already on. It was like an echo of the Lessons from another world, a reflection that made my situation clear.

As we say, Wisdom is a reflection of Knowledge. And when I was a kid, the only knowledge the media showed about black history was about either slaves or pimps—*Roots*, *The Mack*, and that was basically it. So in a way, films like *The Thirty-sixth Chamber* reflected our experience and solidified it, drew people like me into the truth of our own history. And after that, martial arts films became serious to me. I studied them like lessons.

I still do. Even today, if you come to my house you'll see I got a lot of movies there, but about a thousand of them are kung-fu movies. They run from Bruce Lee classics like *The Chinese Connection*, to a John Liu joint like *Secret Rivals*, to *The Hot, the Cool and the Vicious*, which is almost like a Western, to *Martial Arts of Shaolin*, which is one of Jet Li's first films. Today, I watch them for inspiration—to see the hardships Jet Li's character overcomes in *Hero* or *Fearless*, or the trials the family endures in *Curse of the Golden Flower*. I look for signals in my own life, to see how they activate those responses. These films still work that way for me: kung fu, samurai, even anime films—they still act like a mirror.

Take even a cartoon like *Dragon Ball Z*. I mean, it's a cartoon, but it's one of the deepest cartoons in history. Its hero, Son Goku, starts out as a kid, begins martial arts training like San Te, and goes off on a quest for seven balls that unleash dragons that can grant wishes. Now, that's a fantasy, obviously, a children's story. But it's also based on a sixteenth-century Chinese folk novel, about a Buddhist monk who travels to India to find the Buddhist sutras. That voyage represents a journey to enlightenment. But to me, *Dragon Ball Z* also represents the journey of the black man in America.

You see it more clearly as the story goes on. You learn that Son Goku is part of an ancient race called the Saiyans, who come from a distant planet and were known as the fiercest warriors in the galaxy. So Son Goku has superpowers but doesn't realize it—a head injury destroyed his memory, robbed his knowledge of self. Then one day, he gets stressed beyond his limits and Hulks out into his alter ego, Super Saiyan—a nigga with dreadlocks. (Get it?)

This kind of story comes up in world literature, even in the Bible: Abraham is told his seed will be lost for four hundred years, in a land not their own, not knowing who they are or where they're from. That's the story of the Jewish people, but it's also the story of the black man in America.

So I say *we* are the Saiyans; I even use the name Goku as a tag when I write. And when my hair is in an Afro? Word up: I'm Super Saiyan.

By the time I was seventeen, I was going to kung-fu flicks all the time—skipping school, staying out late, hitting the twenty-four-hour movie spots on Forty-second Street, where they showed only porno and kung fu. But then, in 1986, I saw another film that hit me almost as hard as *Thirty-sixth Chamber*. And this one would change many more lives than just my own.

It was a cold night, and Dirty and I were doing like we always did—running around, getting drunk, starting fights, chasing girls. Then finally, around four a.m., we started looking for somewhere warm to crash out with our 40s. We wound up at this funky little porno theater on Forty-second Street and Seventh Avenue, one with a back chamber the size of a classroom, where they showed kung-fu flicks and bums came to sleep. That's what we were about to do, but as we walked in—cold, drunk, and tired—I caught the tail end of a movie that woke me right the fuck up. It ended, another movie started, and I waited up all through that second feature to see the first one again from the beginning. It was called *Shaolin and Wu-Tang,* and I didn't sleep that night.

At that point, I'd have to say this was the best kung-fu movie I'd ever seen. The sword fighting alone was from another planet. Then there was the attitude of the Wu-Tang themselves. The Wu-Tang were defectors from the Shaolin temple, warriors who had trained at Shaolin then developed a sword style that was invincible. In a lot of kung-fu films—like *Fist of the White Lotus* or even *Kill Bill*—the Wu-Tang are actually the *bad* guys. And at one point in *Shaolin and Wu-Tang,* this one Wu-Tang dude defeats thirty Shaolin monks and gets expelled from the temple. Before he goes through, he says: "I may be expelled, but I'm still the best . . . *Wu-Tang!*" Even though he's kicked out of the temple, he's still the baddest motherfucker out there.

That kind of attitude catches on fast in the hood, and pretty soon a lot of Stapleton niggas were onto the Wu-Tang. Then the word was popping up in slang. The first person to use it was Ghost. He'd say "that Wu shit," meaning "that fly shit." He called Old English "Wu juice." But since I was more attuned to the martial arts movies and history, I was able to elaborate: I decided that *I* didn't drink Wu juice—because I drank Ballantine Ale—I drank *Shaolin.* Then I coined the term "Wu-Tang slang," and everybody started speaking it—just as a way to relate to one another.

So before it was a rap group or even a hip-hop crew, Wu-Tang was just a bunch of hustlers living in the hood, guys who loved MCing and hip-hop and connected at my house to make music. A lot of us were in street business to survive, some of us were even enemies. But a love of both hip-hop and the world of knowledge brought us together, and before long we became a brotherhood. To me, that last part came into focus with one final kung-fu film I showed them in 1989, a film that solidified the common love between us.

I had actually seen it years before, with my family. The movie is *Eight-Diagram Pole Fighter*, and it tells a story of a large family that gets betrayed by a general, goes to war, and loses nearly every member to violence. There are eight brothers and three sisters in the film, and I have eight brothers and three sisters in my family. So, in my crib, we all used to watch that together—saw it over and over and over. But a few years later, when I showed it to my friends, it took on a wider, deeper meaning.

By 1989, everyone at the projects was into kung-fu films, and a lot of us had VCRs. So one day, when a bunch of dudes came over to my crib to get high and watch flicks, I pulled out a tape of *Eight-Diagram*. Before we were an hour into it, something strange happened in that crib. People got real quiet, some niggas even started crying. Because that movie is real—it's a reflection of the reality we were all living.

A general betrays a family. A father gets killed. All his sons are killed except for two. One goes crazy. The other shaves his head, becomes a monk. You see this kind of thing happening in the hood every day. We were living in a place torn apart by wars—neighborhood against neighborhood, dealer against dealer—a place where you see people get killed or go crazy every week, a place where the bonds you make are almost stronger than blood. When someone has your back in a situation like that, it's a life-or-death thing—a real brotherhood.

I know that Ghostface, Dirty, and GZA all understood the deeper implication these movies had for our lives, and I know everyone in the Clan does now. From *Thirty-sixth Chamber* you get discipline and struggle. From *Shaolin and Wu-Tang* you get the warrior technique—plus the idea bad guys are sometimes the illest. Then, from *Eight-Diagram Pole Fighter,* you get the brotherhood, the soul. You get the idea that, This guy right here? He's stronger than me. Maybe he can take it a little further than I can. Let me throw my power behind him so we all rise up.

In a way, the group we'd end up forming *had* to be called the Wu-Tang Clan. The name says that we're Wu-Tang warriors, we're from Shaolin, and we're a Clan, which means family. That last part's just as crucial because it's about a connection to something bigger than yourself, which is where the greatest strength always comes from.

That last bit of wisdom started to take hold of me later, when I began studying with Sifu Shi Yan Ming, a thirty-fourth generation Shaolin monk who defected from China in '92 and came to open a Shaolin temple in New York. He was the abbot of his school, I was the abbot of mine—he felt like a peer. But I also wanted to learn from him. "Sifu" can translate as "master," and that's a tough word in the black community, but I realized that sometimes you have to submit to someone to learn. So I did.

With Sifu I learned many Shaolin techniques, but my favorite is probably the Five Elements, maybe because I saw *The Five Deadly Venoms* at a young age. This technique breaks nature down into five basic forces: earth, water, metal, wood, and fire—which are also represented by the kung-fu styles snake, crane, dragon, leopard, and tiger. Most martial arts teach you to be as fluid as water, but earth absorbs water—so you counter water techniques with earth techniques, which absorb blows. Then if someone comes at you with earth techniques, you counter with wood styles, which drive forward. Then you counter wood with metal styles, which chop like an axe, and metal with fire styles, which are more explosive, and, finally, you fight fire with water.

These principles are both external and internal. Internally, it applies to your five major organs. Earth is the spleen, metal is the lungs, water is the kidneys, wood is the liver, fire is the heart. Like, I have asthma, so the form I learned to combat it with was metal—to strengthen my lungs. At the same time, if you have a problem with your lungs, since fire melts metal you think of the energy from your heart pouring into your lungs. If your heart is aching emotionally, you think of the water from your kidney coming to quench your heart. You do all this mentally—it's inner Taoism.

Studying with Sifu, I learned that kung fu was less a fighting style and more about the cultivation of the spirit. What made a Shaolin monk so tough was his mastery of chi—the fact he could make contact with the Earth and draw the energy from it through him. He's using his body, his breath, and his mind to align himself with the Tao—which is pure energy, the energy that sprang from a primal stillness called wu-chi. Tai chi translates as "the grand extreme" and breaks all ideas, forces, and objects into opposites, yin and yang. But wu-chi, which translates as "no extremes," came before tai chi. It's infinite, the source of all power, and it's all one.

A lot of people in our culture see life in terms of opposites—like, good versus evil, me versus you, valuable versus worthless, black versus white. Taoists believe you have to see beyond these to find their essential union. When Wu-Tang Clan started out, we had the saying "Tang is the slang, Wu is the way." I didn't know the tai chi meaning of it then, but it turns out I was on the money. In a way, Wu-Tang pointed me to a wisdom that unified Mathematics and Taoism, that showed me their essential harmony.

Islam is not a religion. It's a way of life in touch with the universe. It's the same as the Tao, which means the Way—it's the way of the universe. The only differences between Taoism and Islam are the more esoteric ideas and traditions that developed around them. True Taoists don't talk about different gods. True Buddhists don't teach various deities. And the basic principle is really the same for Taoism, Buddhism, and Mathematics—to be one with the universe, one with God. They are all the Way.

I think we're all trying to get to one destination—unifying with God. We're all striving to do that here on earth. So when Jesus says, through me you can find the kingdom of heaven, to me, that means he was in tune with God. If you follow his example, you'll find the kingdom of God on earth. We all have natural things in us that prevent us and that help us. We all have evil nature in us—lying, stealing, killing—and we fight against it. The Ten Commandments aren't commandments that you need to read. They're inside you. Islam, Taosim, the teachings of the Bible—they're all ways to get in touch with God's truth within you. And for a lot of people, this takes work.

Look at it this way. In kung-fu training, chambers are the stages of learning you must pass through. But as Mathematicians, we conceive of each chamber as having ten degrees—like the ten degrees in the Lessons. So within each chamber, you go from 1, which represents Knowledge, to 9, which represents Born, like the nine months it takes to bear a child. But then, when you go *past* Born—from 9 to 10—you're actually going back to 1, or Knowledge, because 10 is 1 with a circle beside it.

This kind of thing takes years of meditation to understand, but it's right there beneath the surface, represented in signs and numbers. An enlightened man sees that there actually *are no* numbers. It's all a circle. On a number line, the numbers left of zero head off to negative infinity and the ones right of zero head off to positive infinity. But it's infinity either way. The number line goes in both directions, endlessly, all within that one cycle or chamber. It's the same thing as yin and yang—with a drop of yin there's always a speck of yang—but they all go back to 1.

Today, some brothers get mad at me saying things like this. They say, "Why you fuckin' with Chinese dudes? How come you talk to Caucasian motherfuckers like they're brothers?" I know how they feel. And I bear witness that Allah is one, the Father of the black man, who must take his proper place as God of himself. But over the years, I came to believe the basic lesson of Mathematics is the same as that of Taoism, Buddhism, and every great spiritual path. It's that we all have the potential to become like God.

Even Son Goku eventually learns how to develop chi on his own, to become Super Saiyan at will. And today, I believe we've all got a Saiyan inside us, because God is in each of us. That's what we're all trying to reach, through all the chambers of our lives.

If you reach the thirty-sixth chamber, you have completed your learning. You have multiplied one chamber by 36 and gotten 360 degrees—a completed circle. If you add 3 to 6 you get 9—which represents Born—but then you must add one more to 9, and Born becomes Knowledge again. And this puts you right back into the circle, back at 1.

From Knowledge to Born, then Born, back to Knowledge—it always returns to the beginning, to 1. And right there, that may be the most important lesson you can get. It's Mathematics, baby: We're all one.

But in this world, that kind of thing can take decades to see clearly. Not everyone has that much time, or those opportunities. An ancient Taoist named Ho Shang Kung once wrote, "A dragon is still, thus it can constantly transform itself. A tiger is busy, thus it dies young." And in my life, the tigers would outnumber the dragons ten to one.

HEART

A STREET PARABLE OF COURAGE

When someone is known to be strong in the streets they say, "That nigga got a lot of heart." It doesn't mean he's the toughest dude out there. It just means he has the will and the courage to do something difficult, even if it's just surviving. If he got beat down, he came back up: He got a lot of heart.

But another way of putting that is to say that his soul is large. This relates to the Heart Sutra, one of the shortest but most important sutras in all Buddhist writings. It's from the sutras known as the Perfection of Wisdom and it's only a paragraph long, but you might look at it like the illest rap verse ever spit—simple, tight, and incomparably profound.

Mostly the Heart Sutra is about being able to see reality as it truly is, unclouded by the things human beings project onto it. You read it differently in different translations, but to me, it's about knowing yourself. It's about trusting your heart—real heart, not your ego—to show you the truth. It's about that spark of God inside you. It's a lesson that I learned many years ago, when I was a kid in Staten Island.

When I was thirteen, the toughest guy in my age bracket was a guy they called June-June. June-June matured early—physically he was a man by the eighth grade—and he was also a knockout artist, a bad dude no one wanted to fuck with.

Unfortunately for me, one of the few dudes that *did* fight him was my older brother Divine, who beat him. So when I met June-June a year later in junior high, we had an automatic beef—a sins-of-the-fathers situation. June-June wanted to try me.

In seventh grade, I was one of those dudes who was always going to go for it. Win or lose, I'm going for it every time. So we had a fight, and I have to say he beat me. Put it this way: When you gotta bite a nigga to get up? That means you lost.

I wound up moving to Brooklyn for a year or two and then moved back to Staten Island for high school. And in my first week back in the school, who do I run into? June-June. He was even still with his same little homeboy he'd been hanging with two years ago—a little instigating motherfucker. This little dude said to June-June, "Remember him? Remember him? He's that nigga that bit you that one time." So June-June came up to me and was like, "What up, *boy.*"

By this time, I was fourteen and had knowledge of

myself. And if a man truly knows himself, he also knows his enemy. He knows that even if his enemy is a giant, that giant still has the same weaknesses within him. I think that's why the yin and yang has two dots, one on each side. The dot in your opposite—in this case the bully—is his weak spot. The more knowledge of self you have, the better chance you have of finding that little dot within him. Because that dot is the you in him. It's like Jesus says in the Bible: "How is it that you can see the mote in your brother's eye and not see the beam in your own?" The giant is bullying you for no reason other than that he sees something in you that he sees in himself.

On some level, I perceived that within Infinite. So when he challenged me, I came back at him, saying, "I ain't no *boy*, man." His calling me that meant we had to fight. Again.

This time it happened in McKee Park on Staten Island, between the two high schools, McKee and Curtis. (In a way, they're Wu-Tang feeder schools. U-God went to McKee; I went to Curtis.) June-June and I walked four blocks to go fight in McKee Park, with a crowd following us.

This time we must've fought for an hour. Nobody wins a fight like that. Even though we were only in ninth grade, this was a real fight between two men. There were blood, cuts, the kinds of wounds that don't heal. It ended with him having two rocks in his hands—not a fair fight, if it ever was—and me still not backing down. The fight was over when neither of us could move.

In this case, you would say that we both had heart. I had heart for defending my honor, because in the streets that's all you have. I couldn't beat this guy—he was probably lifting two hundred pounds by this time—but he could not beat me without killing me. I showed heart. And in this case, I showed enough heart that June-June wound up becoming my student. Soon after this, he found Mathematics, took the name Infinite, and began to study with me. I like to think that my heart wanted his respect so I could teach him. That's the good side of heart.

But there's a dark side to heart, and that's ego. That part of heart ended up defeating Infinite.

In a year or two, Infinite became known throughout Staten Island as a tough dude and an egomaniac. A lot of guys that hung with me from Park Hill and Stapleton didn't like him. Infinite was from New Brighton, and a lot of neighborhood wars were started by him and his brother. Mathematics had calmed him down a bit, but he was still knocking niggas out left and right.

You had to say that Infinite had too much of the wrong kind of heart. It got to the point that he was confronted with a life-and-death situation, and ego destroyed him just like it can destroy all of us.

In the kung-fu movie *The Five Deadly Venoms,* there's a character named Golden Arms, who was also called the

Toad, the fifth deadly venom. His style was simply to be invincible. No type of attack, not even blades or spears, could defeat him. You see a lot of Golden Arms kids in the hood—the place brings it out of you—and that's definitely how June-June thought of himself. He was like Golden Arms: "I don't *need* a weapon!"

Infinite beat many men like that.

But eventually he was defeated by a lesser man. That's because he'd already defeated himself. This was a man with one of the biggest hearts in all of Staten Island, but one day he challenged this young nigga with the heart of a coward. He dared this kid to shoot him, and he did. Infinite died. Even the kid who killed him was like, "Yo, I didn't want to kill him. He *made* me." I believe that. I believe it was Infinite's heart that killed him.

They say there's a dark spot in your heart, a tiny black vacuum, that's the size of the tip of a needle. I believe that tiny space is where God is located inside you. That tiny dark spot is a piece of space trapped in our body, something that connects us to the universe and one another. Physics says that nature abhors a vacuum. Whether it's true wisdom or ego, something is going to fill that vacuum in your heart. You'll find out what it is as you go through life.

If you're a young man and have a lot of heart, that means you have courage. But then you learn the other meaning of heart, which is love.

At first, love is a vacuum that takes courage from your

heart. You're scared around a woman you love. You're not the same tough dude, the same thug. At first, love weakens you. But soon it makes you strong in ways you couldn't imagine.

Love is the first two steps, Knowledge and Wisdom, coming together. It's 1 and 2—put them together you get 12, and the twelfth letter in the alphabet is L, which stands for Love. If wisdom is like water, so is love. It dissolves you then rebuilds you stronger. It's like when you have your first child—you've never felt weaker in your life. Your love for that child makes you vulnerable. But it also makes you stronger, because you'll do anything to protect that child. So love, like wisdom, dissolves you and then resolves you. It breaks down your ego and puts you back together again properly.

When love doesn't find its way into your heart, you die. That's what happened with Infinite. His fate was settled by Justice. The tenth letter of the English alphabet is J, and J represents Justice, which breaks down to Just I Ce (or "See") Equality. That means that your reward or penalty after being given Knowledge depends on your way of using it, on how much Wisdom drives your decisions. The universe will show you whether your ego is at the steering wheel or you're using your talent the way God wants you to. It's going to come to light. No matter how much heart you got, it's love you need to survive.

If you don't find love in your heart,
heart will kill you—sooner in the
streets, but eventually everywhere.

The Heart Sutra

Body is nothing more than emptiness,
emptiness is nothing more than body.
The body is exactly empty,
and emptiness is exactly body.

The other four aspects of human existence—
feeling, thought, will, and consciousness—
are likewise nothing more than emptiness,
and emptiness nothing more than they.

All things are empty:
Nothing is born, nothing dies,
nothing is pure, nothing is stained,
nothing increases and nothing decreases.

So, in emptiness, there is no body,
no feeling, no thought,
no will, no consciousness.
There are no eyes, no ears,
no nose, no tongue,
no body, no mind.
There is no seeing, no hearing,
no smelling, no tasting,
no touching, no imagining.
There is nothing seen, nor heard,

nor smelled, nor tasted,
nor touched, nor imagined.

There is no ignorance,
and no end to ignorance.
There is no old age and death,
and no end to old age and death.
There is no suffering, no cause of suffering,
no end to suffering, no path to follow.
There is no attainment of wisdom,
and no wisdom to attain.

The Bodhisattvas rely on the Perfection of Wisdom,
and so with no delusions,
they feel no fear,
and have Nirvana here and now.

All the Buddhas,
past, present, and future,
rely on the Perfection of Wisdom,
and live in full enlightenment.

The Perfection of Wisdom is the greatest mantra.
It is the clearest mantra,
the highest mantra,
the mantra that removes all suffering.

This is truth that cannot be doubted.
Say it so:

Gaté,
gaté,
paragaté,
parasamgaté.
Bodhi!
Svaha!

Gone,
gone,
gone over,
gone fully over.
Awakened!
So be it!

—"Life Changes," Sifu Shi Yin Ming,
in memory of ODB, on *Eight Diagrams*

HOLY WARRIORS

A STREET PARABLE OF FAITH

Whether or not what we experienced was
an according-to-Hoyle miracle is insignificant.
What is significant is that I felt the touch of God.
God *got involved*.

—Jules Winnifield, *Pulp Fiction*

In 1986, New York City hip-hop was a war. As a man is
becoming a samurai, he roams the country in search of
opponents. And as an MC, you did the same thing—
traveling to different neighborhoods to find battles.
Hip-hop at that time was righteous and violent. MCs
were bombing Mathematics *and* murdering foes. I was
seventeen years old and just that kind of walking
contradiction.

I used to ride the subway with a huge, Big Daddy
Kane–style gold cable around my neck, my book of 120
lessons, and a .38 revolver tucked into a slot inside. The
gun and the 120—it's like the Bible and the six-shooter

in a Western, or the sword in a Muslim flag. Human beings have lived with that contradiction for centuries, but Americans always found their own expression of it. And at that time hip-hop gave me a crucial lesson in metaphors and reality, expression and truth.

One night, four buddies and I were at a block party in Manhattan's Lower East Side—five young Muslims, five young street thugs. I was an MC representing All In Together Now Crew, which included GZA and ODB, and we had a mix tape out in the streets by the same name. In a year, I'd put out a record with Tommy Boy as Prince Rakeem—on some smooth, charming-the-ladies-man shit—but for now I was about warfare. The party was in a street park with a baseball field nearby—no stage, just turntables and some equipment. Some other MCs were taking turns, so I jumped right in, rapping "I'm a burn you, nigga . . ."—and I did. I burned 'em up. Then I challenged the DJ on turntables and put work on him as well.

This was a big, loud party, and everyone was Spanish—we were the only black motherfuckers there. So after I burned these MCs down, this one dude got jealous and pulled out a gun. He started talking shit about how *he's* the nicest nigga there and fires into the air—*bam! bam! bam! bam! bam! bam!*—just to help make his point.

You could say that this act made the battle literal. But we didn't care. We were taking mescaline, drinking beer,

and protected by Allah—invincible. So I started talking shit right back. I held up a bag I was carrying and
started laughing—saying, "Nigga, that ain't shit. Don't
let me go in the bag, nigga! Yo, I got the biggest Tec in
the world, nigga! . . ."

In hip-hop and in the streets, a boast is a projection
of strength—a threat that is itself an action. Labor unions
act by *threatening* to strike. Rappers act by *threatening*
to destroy. In fact, whole careers have been based on
pure projection. That was definitely the case here because, in reality, that bag didn't have anything in it but
my lessons and a screwdriver. Even so, my projection
backed that dude down. He started saying, "Nah, nah,
nah—we cool, homie!" We backed him down with the
force of the word.

That was one lesson we should have learned and left
with. Instead, God was going to teach us another.

We were pumped up by this victory and ended up
walking back to the projects—stopping in bodegas, stealing beer, taking whatever we wanted. We must have terrorized this neighborhood for about two hours—talking
to girls, ripping off delis, five cowboys with nothing behind us but this bag.

Then, after about two hours of doing this, I felt like,
"Okay, we're overdoing it." But my man Asaham, who was
my student in Islam, wouldn't stop. "Yo, look at those two
shorties over there," he said. "Let me go holler at them real
quick." He went over and started talking to these girls.

Meanwhile, the bodega people we'd terrorized had been talking to each other. The other dudes from the party were coming back. People were converging around us. But my man was still talking to these two girls. Finally, two guys came walking over to him as we were standing on the side, waiting for him to get their phone numbers. My man yelled to me, "Yo, Ra! These niggas talking shit!" So I had to come over and puff myself up and try my old routine: "Don't let me go to the bag, nigga!"

This time, a little Spanish dude came up, acting all apologetic: "No, no, no, Papi, we don't want no trouble, Papi, we don't want no trouble" and—*BAM!*—punched me in the face. My hat flew off. It was on. In less than thirty seconds, my man Asaham was on the ground, his shoulder broken, and the rest of us were fighting for our lives. As the crowd closed in on us, I tried to front a little bit with the bag—"What, what, what"—but they had real guns out. We'd given them a full two hours to go home and get them.

This was hubris—an overdose of pride, the fatal flaw that gets heroes in Greek epics killed. Which is almost what happened to us. We ran. They started shooting at us. I promise you, unless you've done it, you don't know what it feels like when you hit that corner and hear the fence go *ping! ping! ping!* and see those sparks fly behind you.

Somehow we got away and ended up on some block, out of breath, and realized that one of us, Asaham, was missing. We had to go back for him.

I told my youngest cousin, Richie, to go home, and the three others of us picked up bottles and rocks and started walking back to get Asaham.

As soon as we hit the corner, the mob was right there—at a full run, coming after us. This is when I actually felt that God, and not my own self-projection, saved my life.

I took off my hat and froze. Everybody in that mob ran right by me. None of them saw me, even though I was right in front of them. My friends had left, and I stood there alone and frozen as at least fifteen people ran by. When the last two in the crowd passed, one stopped and looked at me. He said, "Isn't that one of them?" "Nah, nah, nah," the other one said. They ran on. And I took off in the opposite direction.

Three of us made it home that night, with busted heads and broken bones. One of us, Kedar, didn't. He got stabbed thirteen times and spent three weeks in the hospital. This man was a champion fighter, one of the toughest motherfuckers ever—a knockout *master*. He came out in a wheelchair and started walking a year later. He was never the same. It could have been any of us.

I have to give all praises due, because I believe that night, just for a minute, Allah made me invisible. When we held those niggas down for hours with just a screwdriver and the Lessons, that wasn't a miracle. That was a trick. I believe in Jedi mind tricks because I've used them many times. But my invisibility? By taking off my hat and really believing to myself that they didn't see me? That was faith—a desperate faith, a true faith.

When the Meccans were trying to kill Muhammad, he hid in a cave. When his would-be assassins found it, they saw a spiderweb hanging across the entrance, so they didn't go in—they figured no one had broken the web so no one was there.

Scientists have said that a spiderweb, structurally, is stronger than steel. The strongest bulletproof vest you can make is essentially spiderwebs woven together. You measure a molecule of steel versus a molecule of spiderweb, the spiderweb is stronger. I put that in a lyric: "A spiderweb is known to be stronger than steel / Trapped in a cave, Muhammad used it as his only shield." In that moment, my spiderweb was my cloak of invisibility. It was my belief, my faith. It would save my life again.

God is alive within you—terror

and desperation summon His force.

Faith is a pillar of life that many confuse

with hope. It is beyond hope, for hope

can be applied without knowing; faith

is the heart-projected action of

knowing. It's wisdom before

it reaches understanding.

WIT

The first word in one of Wu-Tang's acronyms is *witty*: Witty Unpredictable Talent and Natural Game. That's because wit is a form of wisdom, a form that deflects and absorbs, a kind that can save your life. I learned this lesson during a card game in jail.

We were playing spades, and in jail spades is a very serious game. You deal thirteen cards to each player, and each team tries to win the most "books." You and your partner use strategy and give subtle hints to each other, so it actually gets mad complex and psychological for such a simple game. On top of that, in prison you play for prison stakes—cigarettes, food, whatever—so the stakes are higher than they are outside.

In this one game, me and my partner were playing two other guys for our breakfast. I was probably about three days in, eighteen or nineteen years old—young, skinny, and new. My partner, Mike, was a muscular giant who had been in for a while. He was the kind of nigga you did not want to fuck with—everyone was afraid of Big Mike.

At first, Big Mike and I were playing and communicating with each other well. I'm a good player, and we were doing some work on these other guys; we were busting some ass. But I made a crucial mistake because I didn't know my partner well enough. In a way I lacked the wisdom for this particular game. Our bet was two-for-ten, which is a do-or-die bet. If you make it, you win the game, if you miss, you lose the game—all in a single hand.

Mike threw me a signal that I didn't read. And this one time—on the game-winning hand—I blew it. My mistake led to us losing our hand, our game, and our breakfast. This was bad.

Mike jumped up and got like an animal. "Motherfuckin' Slim, why the fuck didn't you play the diamonds?" He came at me and—*boom*—it was about to be me and him.

I didn't know what to do—I almost came with the violence back at him. But instead of bringing it, I thought of kung fu. I got loud and flipped it.

I yelled, "Man, *fuck* them bitchass niggas, Mike. We gon' get those niggas *next* time!"

In a second, I deflected the beef to the other guys who beat us and reestablished myself as being on Mike's side. We both lost, we both were going to go hungry, and Mike wanted to put hands on me—but I deflected it.

And it worked. Suddenly, Mike chimed in. "Yeah!

Fuck y'all bitchass niggas, we gon' get y'all niggas *next* time." And he gave me a pound. It was a close call. I was saved by wit and wisdom.

It's like Bruce Lee said: "I practice the art of fighting without fighting." He also said, "You don't have to fight the giant every time."

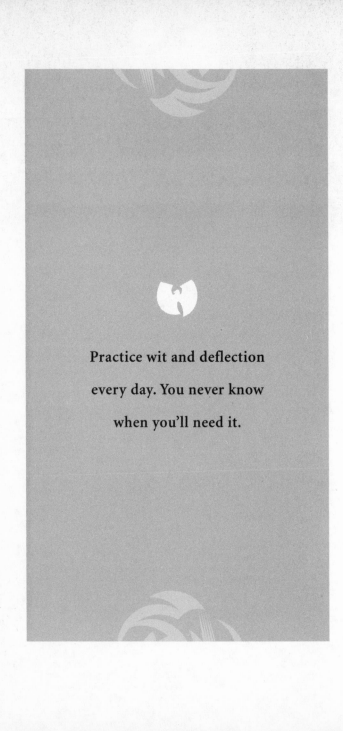

Practice wit and deflection
every day. You never know
when you'll need it.

DARKNESS AND LIGHT

Dear Prince, what is light?
*Light is that force that expels darkness; it is the phenomenon
that darkness brings about.*

What is the brightest form of light?
*The darkest of the black holes, for it is the closest to the state
of darkness in which light was created.*

Dear Prince, your wisdom is truly superb!
*Thank you, minister, it's thanks to your light that I'm able
to see so clearly.*

*In the darkness of the womb exist the atom of life and the
light of Knowledge. It is this light of Knowledge that brought
the light of Wisdom to the light of Understanding to the
Freedom from the darkness in which life was.*

In other words, the knowledge of self is the light that shone in the darkness to detect the atom of life—not life itself, for life has no beginning or ending.

In the atom of life exist the three charges: positive, negative, and neutral, commonly called proton electron neutron. It is the will induced on these charges that says, "Let there be light!" In the darkness of the sperm the light of the knowledge of life exists. The cell duplicates and replicates with the knowledge that has been embedded into it by the will of Allah. All cells have this knowledge by what to do from Allah. His will be done forever, for He shined light on darkness and dispelled it even though from out of darkness light was produced. The Sun has been burning for trillions of years; it must be deepest black, for all things burn black. His will is embedded in all cells and atoms since the first atom moved out of darkness and first life moved out of the womb of darkness.

Even before the mother is in light of the existence of the child, the child is in light of itself. The cells begin forming once the divine union is sparked by the sperm and egg from within the light of itself and knowledge of its job and in submission to the will of Allah the Father to all and Lord of all the Worlds.

The voyage of the best ship is a
zigzag line of a hundred tacks.

—RALPH WALDO EMERSON

Outside Pittsburgh, along the Ohio River, there's a
town called Steubenville, Ohio. It's a weird place,
with a long history of political and police corruption
and lots of rumors and legends surrounding it. Some
people know it as the birthplace of Dean Martin. Others,
like members of a Trinity church there, believe it will be
the site of Jesus Christ's Second Coming. For me, Steubenville represents darkness—a darkness that I made for
myself, a darkness that almost took me for good.

For a few years, my cousins Ghost and Dirty and I
would come down to Steubenville from Staten Island
to visit family. I made my first trip down there at nineteen, and that time I came with righteousness. I brought
my book of Lessons and started teaching Mathematics
to anyone who wanted to learn. Before long I had about
twenty students. We'd meet every day at the town library, and soon our group got so big that they moved us
to a community center. Then other community leaders

started showing up, and we began running roundtable discussions. We talked about the Divine Mathematics, but also geometry, biology, and all sorts of other subjects. It was like a seminar of the streets.

Some people at those meetings came from other street schools, like Universal Law, which, like Mathematics, was taught in prison. Every jail, whether it's in Ohio, New York, or L.A., has some form of these studies. Somebody gets hold of them and adapts them to their own sect. The Black Panthers—they had precepts. The Mah-Wahs—they had precepts. Even the Bloods have lessons now. And all of them draw on either Islam, Christianity, or the Jehovah's Witnesses. Each one takes the precepts and twists them in different ways to help teach and empower young guys who are thirsty for knowledge. It's one of the few benefits of prison—letting teachers and students form a community of learning.

Ours was called the Five Percent—for the Five Percent Nation of Islam—but I would say the name applies globally and historically as well. Anyone dedicated to freedom, justice, and equality is what we call a poor righteous teacher. These are part of that 5 percent of any given society who know the truth and will speak it freely without personal gain. Gandhi was a Five Percenter. Martin Luther King Jr. was a Five Percenter. Jesus was a Five Percenter. The Shaolin monks and their disciples, the Taoist priests and the Confucians—they're the Five Percenters of China.

When I first went down to Steubenville, I came as a true member of the Five Percent. And the knowledge I shared took root. Some of my students formed the Wu-Tang offshoots Fourth Disciple and Killer Army. Some of them had some success, some went back to being street thugs, but at least my first trip down to Steubenville was righteous. My second trip was the exact opposite.

Around 1991, things were bad for us in New York. My album as Prince Rakeem wasn't paying my bills. GZA's record for Cold Chillin' didn't do well either. We needed money, one of my friends got killed, some people were trying to kill me, and all of us were just scrambling.

Ghost was doing things like waiting outside a stop for the Brinks truck, trying to figure a way to rip them off. Or we'd wait outside drug dealers' houses—saying, "When he comes out in his Benz, we'll put a gun in his face, take his Benz, and go sell it." None of this would have worked, but we were desperate. So I went back to the street game. I began chopping nicks up to sell them and started thinking: *I know a place where they aren't as advanced in this game, a place where we could go out and get a hustle on.* And that's what we did. We headed back to Steubenville.

I borrowed some money from GZA and gave it to Ghost—because Ghost was already a street vendor—and said, "Ghost, go get what we need." He did a robbery—robbing someone we know, that's how bad it was—and we headed down to Ohio. This time, I'm on the Amtrak with a briefcase holding my product, a gun, and my Lessons—and wearing a gold chain to pawn for cash flow. This time we went down and we got into hell.

Before we got down there Steubenville's nickname was Little Chicago. After we got established there it became known as Little New York. We made money and were able to feed ourselves, but it was the most negative point in my life. This was the time I broke my one vow to myself. I never wanted to be a drug dealer—I thought I was killing my own people—but for my own survival I entered that world. I betrayed myself.

A lot of bad things happened quickly. A lot of street beefs developed from us moving in. And before long my brother was in jail, Dirty was in jail, I was in jail, Ghost got shot, and my student Wise got shot. We came apart as individuals. And I found myself on trial for attempted murder.

I had gotten dragged into a beef between a girl Ghost was seeing and her man's crew. I was driving that girl and her friend home one night—Ghost wasn't even in town—and some of those dudes pulled up next to us at a stoplight. They were street hustlers—everybody was then—and this one guy sees his girl in a car and goes into a jealous rage.

Before I left the house, I had been given one commandment from my sister: "You better not fuck my car up." But at the light, this nigga jumps out and starts kicking the car, bashing the windows, denting it. The girls start screaming, "Drive, drive, he got a gun!"—so I pull out and he starts chasing me. I zipped out, got away, and laid low for a while.

In a couple hours, I took them home, but the one girl lived on a dead-end street. She got out and went into her house, but those same guys were parked there waiting for us in an ambush. Immediately, it was pandemonium: A lot of shots were fired, my car was still moving, crashed up on the sidewalk, and everyone was pulling their shit out, yelling, "Fuck you!" "Nah, fuck you!" In the end, it wasn't really that big a deal—there probably ended up being just six or seven shells on the ground—but that scuffle got me charged with attempted murder.

The fact is, the charge I was facing did not fit the offense. The actual incident was a case of self-defense. I regret that somebody got shot and I felt bad for being a part of that kind of violence. I would have copped out to sixty days; I would have copped out to a year. But the prosecutor wanted eight years—he wanted to nail me down. This is when things started to become clear to me. One, I gained clarity about our legal system—its unfairness of matching crime and punishment. But two, I gained clarity about my life.

On top of everything else, I had gotten my girlfriend pregnant. I was in jail for thirty days and started thinking about this, how I had a baby girl coming, how I had to change my life. That's why I named my daughter Ra-Mecca—"Ra" to signify me, Rakeem, and "Mecca" to represent the Holy City, the highest point, the beginning. She would be the highest achievement of my life so far. I knew then what I'd be losing.

So I prepared. I stopped smoking, stopped drinking, started studying the Lessons again. I thought about my daughter having to visit me for eight years inside—because I didn't think I was gonna win this case. And when I finally bailed out, I was in the law library every day. In fact, I used to run into the judge and the prosecutor there. They'd see me and mean-mug me, as if they were thinking, *What's this guy doing sitting there?*

Finally, the day of the trial came. It was a three-day trial and ended on April 22. That was the day my lawyer put me on the stand. In a way, I gave the most important performance of my life that day, and it was from the heart. I addressed the jury myself—told my story, presented it vividly, gave testimony as powerfully as I could. Then the jury, which had only one black guy on it, went away and deliberated. They were gone for two hours and came back. I was nervous; my stomach was going crazy. And the woman read the verdict: "Not guilty."

I can't really explain the feeling in the courtroom at that moment. I mean, obviously *I* was ecstatic, but some of the people on this jury were *crying.* Two old white women and a white man came up and hugged me. There was even an article in the paper that said something like "Jury Cries as Diggs Sentence Comes." And as

I left the stand, my mother says, "This is your second chance."

That day, I got eight years of my life back in my own hands. I realized, *Oh, it's me? I'm the man? I'm the one who can fix my life?* I decided to take real control of my music career. I went back to Staten Island and called Tommy Boy, but they were done with me. Whatever was going to happen was going to happen outside that system. And I realized the first step was to reclaim myself.

Down in Steubenville, we used different code names. Ghost was Moses and I was Jesus—an irony we both appreciated at the time. But after the trial, I got back into Prince Rakeem.

I named myself Rakeem at the age of eleven, when I found Knowledge of Self. I renamed myself Prince Rakeem when I mastered the 120. Then Divine Prince Rakeem. Then by the time I was eighteen, and had ten or more students of my own, I named myself Divine Prince Master Rakeem Allah. But through dealing with negativity, I lost that persona. So after the Ohio event and all the chaos it brought to my life, I had to bring that title back. I had to rejoin the Five Percent.

The laymen, the people who don't know much and are easily misled—they're the 85 percent. Those who know the truth but use it to deceive and exploit—they're the 10 percent. You see the 10 percent everywhere today, in every news broadcast, on the front page of every paper.

You know their names. And their crimes are only getting greater, the pain they inflict more widespread.

So when people say the Five Percent is just a gang, I say they're just seekers and givers of knowledge, which is exactly what we need right now. Our culture is programming its children to join the 85 percent, to be robots, to have no knowledge of self. Today, being one of the 85 percent might mean being married in the suburbs with 2.5 kids and 3 cars, spending your days eating prepackaged food, and talking about ten-year-old sitcoms. It might mean chasing Escalades, Rolexes, and power in a corporation that will betray you. It might mean simply accepting everything you see without question. Today, we need some form of the Five Percent. We need people to teach civilization to all the human families. Money gives you economic freedom, but it doesn't free your dome from the lies and ignorance that make you dumb.

I had become dumb. My life had done a zigzag. I was in the right place from ages eleven to sixteen. Then I got involved with women, drugs, and hip-hop in a street way—not just a hobby way where you're having fun in your house, but a street way, with battling, guns, cars, gold cables, drug using, and drug dealing.

This is a man who already had enlightened twenty other kids. Ason Unique—who became Ol' Dirty Bastard—he was a student of mine. I had other students in Brownsville, in Bed-Stuy—*they* knew the 120 now. Now my students were teachers. And here I am—someone who knew the 120 before he was thirteen—here I am acting like a fucking savage? I had to change—change back.

In the Divine Alphabet, Z stands for Zig-Zag-Zig, which means Knowledge, Wisdom, and Understanding. It's the last letter of the alphabet and represents the final step of consciousness. So finally I just thought of the name as letters, as a title, not just a word. R-Z-A. It stands for Ruler-Knowledge/Wisdom/Understanding-Allah.

In my life, I was zigging. I was going right but I zagged. I zagged and I almost died zagging. So I zigged back. I became the RZA. Rakeem Zig-Zag-Zig Allah. Later, people came to call me the RZA-rector—like I bring people back to life. But that year I found out the truth: The first person you have to resurrect is yourself.

Forces in the world will tell you
you're a victim—of your family,
your race, your past, your history.
Don't believe them. They don't know
you. Look inside and find your true
self. It's there. Give it a name.

ABOVE THE RUCKUS

A GUIDE TO KNOWLEDGE OF SELF

Fast for a few days. Don't have a lot of people around. Be alone and quiet. You'll start to hear yourself, feel yourself. You'll hear from the you that's not the you your family, society, or history created. You'll hear from the you that's beneath that, the one that's always there with you—the you that contains the God particle.

Take time. This country fills up every second of your day with noise. That's why they call this place Babylon—the Great Harlot, the Great Deceiver. Because it keeps us away from our true selves. So do the one thing this culture tries hard not to let you do: Look inside yourself.

Be by yourself. Yell out asking God for help until you're almost crying. Let all those chemicals inside you come rushing up to your brain and ask for whatever you're looking for. This is prayer—it's opening your heart.

Martial arts are a form of prayer—they're why Da'Mo taught the monks kung fu. The monks were getting tired and sleepy and couldn't pray properly, so Da'Mo taught them certain postures to strengthen their bodies. Same goes with the Muslims. They weren't in shape, their diet was bad—they weren't in good condition to pray. So the Prophet taught them how to do Salaat, the Islamic prayer rituals that are basically martial arts. (In fact, one long form actually looks like the kung-fu style Sleeping Lo-Han.)

Find a form of prayer and do it—to enhance your life, build up your chi, to attract positivity. Studying lessons and reading great religious books is an excellent form of prayer. But whichever you choose, don't pray to have something pop up under your Christmas tree. Pray to put yourself in harmony with God. Do that and your prayers will be answered.

Don't pray for a thing.

Pray to put yourself in

harmony with God.

ENTER THE ABBOT

What we learn to do
we learn by doing.

—ARISTOTLE

In April of 1991, I got back to New York on a mission. At my trial, my moms inspired me to walk the right path, and I did—literally. In Staten Island, I walked every day for hours. I mean, *walked*, like Da'Mo walked all the way from India to China. I'd walk from the Park Hill projects to the Staten Island ferry dock, from New Brighton to the Stapleton projects, walking through May, June, July. Some people thought I was crazy because they'd see me out there walking and talking to myself. Later, I told one of them, "I may have been talking, but I wasn't talking to myself."

Those walks were a form of meditation, which any

wisdom seeker should practice. You can meditate in the lotus position—the "royal seat" or the "royal crown" position, as it's called—or you can meditate just walking down the block. You don't have to be still; your eyes don't have to be closed. Meditation just means you are aware of your inner self as well as your outer self. Watch yourself, because nobody else is gonna watch you but you.

Like most meditation, those walks on Staten Island didn't create something; they revealed something—something that was already floating over the island, ready to take form. I found that what I wanted to do, could do, and should do was form a record company, collect the best MCs I knew, and become the kind of rap group that no one had ever imagined.

Meditation allowed me to see what we already were in a new light. It brought me Wisdom—which is light. It illuminated how these seemingly unrelated areas of knowledge connected to one another. For example, I'd been reading the Bible for years. When it says that Peter cut the guy's ear off in the garden, I figured that Peter had to be a martial artist. To cut a guy's ear off with a slice that precise you gotta be *nice.* That's on a physical level. But on a mental level, his *words* were that nice. He must have said something that wrecked this guy with his knowledge. That kind of knowledge could work in hip-hop.

The knowledge was latent—the Wu-Tang movie, the Bible stories, the kung-fu epics, hip-hop battles—but meditation allowed me to connect them all, to see their possibilities and apply them to my life. Knowledge is knowing, wisdom is doing. And I realized that nobody else could do that at the time, because nobody had that particular group of experiences, knowledge, and homies. I'd been making tapes with these dudes for years. Even when I had a deal as Prince Rakeem, Park Hill niggas like Meth, Deck, Raekwon, and U-God would come over to my crib, and I'd produce them. But meditations on Staten Island revealed what was there the whole time: the illest MC team in history.

When Da'Mo was meditating for nine years, his future self came back and talked to his current self. His current self said, "Who are you?" his future self says, "I'm you." And Da'Mo says, "What do you mean?" His future self says, "I'm what you're going to become." Da'Mo had attained a state in which he could see that time is linear but life is eternal. So there's really no beginning, no ending. Linear logic measures only the four dimensions: length, width, depth, and time. But in the fifth dimension, energy surpasses time. Light surpasses time. Time is just a controller of certain planes. It's not the master.

The true master is consciousness, and I mean *true* consciousness—not simply being awake—I'm talking about the consciousness that never sleeps. The part of you that is aware of your consciousness. There's a part of you that's always there, always consistent, that represents your true self—the part connected to God. *That's* who you gotta get in touch with.

In my case, I wouldn't say I had that mythic dimension that Da'Mo had, but I definitely had those moments of seeing ahead. I was blessed with that sight. To this day, I feel that's what gave me the vision that drove me through that year—what removed obstacles, guided actions, and brought us all together.

It was't easy. I moved to 134 Morningstar Road in Staten Island, a two-bedroom place I shared with my girlfriend, our daughter, Ghost, my brother Divine, my brother Born, and my sister Sherri. It was the first address for Wu-Tang Productions. My girlfriend, my daughter, and I slept on the floor on a boxing-gym mat. There I felt a force larger than me, larger than any of us, that was calling our group into being.

You could feel it in our first talk about forming a crew—a talk that saved Method Man's life. I was talking with Rae about the idea outside a building called 160—160 Park Hill Avenue, the building in our first video, for "Protect Ya Neck." It was our hangout spot and the drug spot, a center of life and death. I was across the street from 160 talking with Rae, Deck, and a few other homies about forming a crew called the Wu-Tang Clan. Then I saw Method Man coming down the sidewalk.

I yelled over to him, "Yo, Shaquan"—then he was known as Shaquan—"Shaquan! Come over here, yo!" He was on his way into 160 to score some weed. But when he heard me, he stopped and came running over. A few seconds later—*pow-pow-pow-pow-pow!*—a guy started shooting up the front of 160. A buddy of ours, Poppy, an innocent, school-going, nice guy—he was shot and killed right there. The guys who shot him were Brooklyn niggas beefing with Staten Island niggas—they were gunning for Meth. Meth later told me, "Yo, you saved my life that day, because I was headed right into the doorway that got shot up."

There was a kind of fate, this kind of universal momentum behind us then, and it helped me do something no one else had done—unite eight talented, unique, individual MCs as one.

At first the Clan was just me and Ghost, though everyone else was down with Wu-Tang crew and Wu-Tang slang, but it was more like a street gang than a group. I'd signed most of them to my production company. Dirty and my GZA were my cousins so they were down. Method Man and Deck signed as my two main artists. But this time, at Morningstar Road, I called all the brothers together. I said that we were going to go out as Wu-Tang Clan.

I had the contracts ready. I said give me five years and I will take us to number one. It was a long conversation, eye-to-eye, man-to-man. I said that no one could question my authority. It had to be a dictatorship. I didn't say I was the toughest nigga in the crew, but with what I had in mind, I had to be the so-called leader because I was the best *knower*. The best leader is somebody who's able to serve. If you're truly able to serve, you're able to lead. I think the other members of the Clan could see that in me.

I was a bit older than some of them. I was known to be a good knower—the youngest to master the 120—and they always looked at me as an intelligent guy in the neighborhood who never crossed any of them. In a way, I led by example. Even when I was involved with negativity, I think they could see that I never did it with a negative heart. I did it out of desperation.

Everyone agreed and everyone signed the contract. In October of 1992, we recorded the single of "Protect Ya Neck" and started selling out of the trunk of my cousin Mook's Mercury Scorpio—no record deal, no support. It wasn't until December or January that New York's WBLS played it, on Kid Capri's show. Most of us were all on Morningstar Road, packing records up and listening to BLS, when it came for the first time. Raekwon jumped so high into the air—and he's short—that his head almost hit the ceiling. I'll never forget that moment. Our record was on the fucking radio.

After that happened, I started taking meetings, trying to get deals. It was time to enter the music business for real. And I gotta say, when I came, I came in war. I did not come in peace. I came in with the Wu-Tang sword and my own army—but it was an army that I loved.

As hip-hop kept growing as a movement, a lot of people became successful because they started forming alliances with other celebrities—now, you'll see a song with five or six celebrities all from the South, but with individual careers. But they weren't childhood friends.

We were all childhood friends. We were a clan, for real. And this shaped our business dealings. There's a Chinese proverb that says, "When planning for a year, plant corn. When planning for a decade, plant trees. When planning for life, train and educate people." I felt we were planning for life.

By March of '93, "Protect Ya Neck" had sold over ten thousand singles. That got our names on the radar of some record execs, one of them being Steve Rifkind, head of Loud Records. Rifkind offered Wu-Tang a single deal with an album option. While there were other labels that wanted to sign us—some offering as much as $200,000—most of them wanted to sign the group as a whole, including any solo efforts. But I knew that a sum like two hundred grand wouldn't be enough money to support us and keep us going on the long-term plan I had for us. So instead we signed with Rifkind for a fraction of the money, but with the freedom to solicit ourselves to other labels and make solo deals.

After signing with Loud, we decided to replace the song "After the Laughter Comes Tears" from the B-Side of "Protect Ya Neck" with the single "Method Man." We re-recorded "Method Man," improved the quality, and put it out. That single took off—by April, thirty thousand copies had been sold, becoming Rifkind's biggest single so far. As the Abbot, I felt it was wisest for the Clan to invest in Method Man as a solo artist—a decision the Clan agreed with—knowing that the song would be huge enough to make Method Man a star. In fact, that became my primary objective: to systematically launch each member as a solo star by giving them exposure through the Wu-Tang Clan—a crucial part of my five-year plan.

The success of "Method Man" and the buzz around Wu-Tang caused other labels to come checking for us. One of them was Def Jam, the label every rapper wanted to be signed to—the epitome of hip-hop on the East Coast. Naturally, we were excited when Def Jam's A&R rep, Tracy Waples, came out to Morningside Road, listened to our music, went back and told Russell Simmons about us. In fact, Simmons wanted to sign both Method Man and Dirty. But I didn't want to put both artists on the same label. My idea was to spread it out and I had recently called Elektra Records and spoken to the A&R rep Dante Ross, who was in love with ODB. So Method Man went to Def Jam, ODB—unwillingly—went to Elektra, and the Wu-Tang sound began to be dispersed throughout the industry.

We finished the Wu-Tang Clan album *Enter the Wu-Tang 36 Chambers*. It came out in November 1993 and sold thirty thousand units in its first week. It cost exactly $36,000 to make. Of course it did. It was our thirty-sixth chamber. After all those years of being confined to Staten Island, developing talent, going through the training of the chambers, this was our moment to share our wisdom with the world. That's why we chose the name Wu-Tang instead of Shaolin. Shaolin is a holy place—there's no violence or crime in Shaolin. Wu-Tang are the people who studied at Shaolin and left. Some of them joined the government, some became killers, others bandits; in some movies they're good guys, but mostly they're bad. I thought we were the bad guys but that we were bringing this Shaolin chamber to the world. That's why I named Staten Island Shaolin. While Shaolin stayed on Staten Island, Wu-Tang went out into the world.

Wu-Tang Clan truly did take a martial arts approach to hip-hop—to the sound of the music, the style of the lyrics, the competitive wordplay of the rhyming, the mental preparations involved. I think we really did bring a new school to the world. But for one of us, the study in Shaolin wasn't complete. I was still in the temple, still in my final chambers of hip-hop production.

I'd been there for years, making my own beats since around '82. Me and my big brother Divine were hip-hop fiends and, in a way, electronic geeks as well. We always had our own turntables, our own echo box, our own microphones, our own four-track recorders. For me, it came from a burning passion to make my own songs.

In '82, I started out with a straight-arm Technics SL-6 turntable. By '85, I had a Roland 606 drum machine, then a 707. By '88, I got my first sampler, a little Casio toy that sampled only two seconds of sound at a time. I was always scrambling for new gear—borrowing, stealing—but I didn't do it out of love of technology. I did it out of love of hip-hop. I was the guy who used to break-dance, DJ, write graffiti, MC—do anything to do with hip-hop. That's probably one of the reasons the title abbot stuck with me. Because I was a student of all forms.

At certain points in your education, it's good to be focused, to be a purist. In a way, that's what I was, a hip-hop purist, but a purist of hip-hop in its entirety. Back then not all hip-hop producers, certainly not the most famous, were that deeply into all aspects of hip-hop culture. You look at someone like Heavy D—he's a great, platinum-selling artist, but his beats sound more like booty-shaking music. Afrika Bambaataa, he's a founder of hip-hop and deserves supreme respect, but he and his crew dressed like George Clinton, and their music was funkier and more dance-oriented. But I felt there was an actual sound to hip-hop culture then, a spirit that existed on its own plane, in the streets and parks, in the air. I wanted to be a vessel for that sound.

Me and my crew were strictly hip-hop. I hated anything else. I made beats to rhyme to, not to make a party jump. You look at Rob Base, "It Takes Two," that was a number-one record, but he wasn't a good MC, and no good MC ever made a good song with that beat. On the other hand, KRS-One was an MC. His beats weren't club-rocking beats; it was his lyrics that made the club rock. Or look at Eric B. and Rakim. Their song "Eric B. Is President" was a club rocker, but the song that made everyone really notice Rakim as an MC was "My Melody." On the *radio* you heard, "I came in the door, I said it before . . ." from "Eric B. Is President." On the *streets* you heard, "I take seven MCs, put 'em in the line . . ." from "My Melody." That was the actual *sound* of hip-hop.

That's what I strove to make: street music, beats that MCs could rap on, beats that would make you wanna rip a hole out of the wall. I was focused. But it took a while for people to catch on to what I was trying to do, and for me to realize that a true artist is a craftsman, someone who knows the art from the bottom up.

When I was MCing as Prince Rakeem, my manager would take me to all these different producers to make songs. I'd got all over New York—the Bronx, Harlem, Manhattan—listen to fifty beats before I found one I wanted to rhyme to. Finally, I told him, "Can you buy me a beat machine and let me make the beats?" He said, "Nah." He thought my beats were weird; he didn't think I had it.

After I got kicked out of the Stapleton projects, I wound up in an apartment at 7 Purroy Place, upstairs from my aunt, right around the corner from my grandmother's place on Targee. This was a starving-artist situation. I had to plug my equipment into my aunt's downstairs apartment through a long extension cord so I could have electricity for lights and making beats. But Meth and I recorded the song "Method Man" there. I made the beat for "Wu-Tang Clan Ain't Nuthin' to Fuck With" there. All of it was done with stolen electricity, on a little eight-track, an Emulator X SP1200 sampler, and an Ensoniq EPS 16 Plus sampling keyboard that I got from hustling. It was the true hip-hop means of production.

After that, we moved to Morningstar Road, to a two-bedroom shared by seven people, where we made the beat and most of the song for "C.R.E.A.M." Then, when we started making money off our first singles, I moved my girl and baby to a two-bedroom in Michelle Court, in Staten Island's Mariners Harbor. That's where I feel I completed my training in hip-hop production—where I truly mastered the craft.

The music on *36 Chambers* is an accumulation of beats from the Stapleton projects, Purroy, and Morningstar Road. But at Michelle Court, I found something I never had in my life: a basement. I put studio equipment down there, and from that moment I was down there all day, every day. I made beats for everybody. I put them all on floppy discs, put a sticker with each MC's name on it, each one on a floppy disc I filled with beats for their solo albums: 20 discs for Meth, 20 for Ghost—over 150 discs.

I had completed many chambers in production training by the time I moved into this basement. After Method Man's *Tical* went platinum in its first few months, the publishing deal landed me a lot of money. But instead of buying a car or whatever rap stars were supposed to do, I turned that basement from a beat laboratory into a fully independent studio, a place we could complete entire albums. This is where I had my steepest learning curve, in the years 1994–96.

This place became a dojo—Japanese for "place of the Tao"—a space for gathering, training, spiritual growth. It might not have looked it. All we did in that basement was make music, smoke weed, and cook turkey burgers. You'd hear burgers frying, chess games going, and the video game Samurai Showdown being played. But everything else was music.

When I bought my first house, in Cleveland, Ohio, I sent my family there, but I stayed in New York to live and work. I didn't come out of that basement for years, literally. Scientists have said that it takes ten thousand hours of practice to become a master. I'd been making hip-hop music since I was thirteen, but down in this laboratory I probably rounded out the last few of those ten thousand, recording, mixing, studying, creating—learning. In that basement I made ODB's *Return to the 36 Chambers*, Raekwon's *Only Built 4 Cuban Linx,* and GZA's *Liquid Swords*—all in '95.

When we did *Tical* and *36 Chambers* in Manhattan studios, I always felt the demos sounded better than the final product. There was a rawness missing. I also felt that the established engineers I was working with didn't know what they were doing when it came to my music. So I decided that I had to set up everything where no one would hear it, no one would engineer it, but me. And that's what I did.

When we worked on *Cuban Linx,* there was no engineer. Not a single knob was twisted by anyone but me. When we did *Killah Army, Sons of Man*—we did all these albums in that basement, without spending any money. Later, I heard some people say they thought I was being egotistical when I had the albums say, "mixed, produced, and arranged by the RZA." They'd say, "He doesn't know how to mix; he doesn't know how to arrange; he's not an engineer." They didn't know that I knew every single board function in and out. I had to. By the time we were doing *Cuban Linx,* I was at one with the producer's medium.

Producing music is like playing an instrument—it's an expression of yourself. Every pianist touches the keys differently, every violinist bows based on the strength of their arm, the structure of their hand. That's why Miles Davis is one of the greatest players, because of the spirit that he blows through that trumpet. It's his. Creativity is always unique, because it's you. It's the same thing with producing—you have to sit there, find yourself in the sound.

You don't need someone asking you "You want some more bass on your kick?" or giving you a scientific explanation of how it should be. A lot of engineers went to school for this, so they'll tell you, "If the vocals are at two kilohertz, your snare should be either above that or below that so it doesn't clash with the vocals." But I found that sometimes the snare *has* to clash with the vocals to punctuate them. You have to ignore the science of it, even the logic of it. Sometimes real discoveries take a leap in consciousness that's outside the intellect.

One thing I discovered was that you could have ten unrelated things playing at the same time, as long as each was at the right amplitude. So even though the track might not be on beat, because of the volume level of the drums, the pulse forces everything to fall on beat. That way can put one thing at a tempo of 100 beats per minute, another at 20, another at 150, with the drums going at a steady tempo of 95. Everything else—it might be strings, a bass sample from a Stax record, a sample from a Russian choir—can be made to fall into place. You use a synthesizer to pick out certain notes and frequencies from the samples, to bring that out of the mix, to let the ear tune into that, to create a form. In a song like "4th Chamber," the melody line of the keyboard is what makes the other noise stick together.

One day, one of my students, a producer named True Master, noticed something. We were in the studio, and he accidentally hit a fader and the whole beat fell apart. Just one fader, one track, one instrument—and the whole thing fell into chaos. Another time, he was listening to me mixing a song—just kicking back, smoking weed, and listening—and he kept pointing to one line that was off. "That's off, that's off," he'd say, pointing to the fader of one track. And when I finished balancing everything, he realized that it was only off until it was balanced.

That's the whole secret to it: It's off, but it isn't off. It's off and on at the same time.

Music only needs a pulse. Even just a hum will force a pulse, a beat. It makes order out of noise. It'll work with anything. I think that's what true producing is: *finding* music. You listen and you can hear it.

Today, making music, making beats—it's like breathing for me. I have thousands of beats I'll probably never release, but I can't stop making them any more than I can stop breathing. You're a vehicle for your breath, and I'm a vehicle for the music breathing through me. If you look at more of your daily creativity like that, it helps you to be more productive. You get out of the way. The kung-fu principle of *wu-wei* teaches us how to act without action. In the phrase, the word *wu* translates as "without." It means that you use the power of the universe but use it without effort, bring yourself into balance with the flow of life. It's a daily thing, an hourly thing.

A few floors above my basement in the town house, family members of the Queens hip-hop group Organized Konfusion were living. I remember Prince Po used to come around and check me out making beats and rhymes. It's funny that I'd be visited by a member of Organized Konfusion because that's exactly what I was practicing a couple floors below: organized confusion. I was making music, but I was also practicing something spiritual. I was trusting chaos and confusion—not judging it, not fearing it, not reaching for an immediate solution. That's not just a secret to production. It's a secret to life.

You and your life—it has a consistency, no matter what you go through. You just have to be detached enough to recognize the good and the bad in yourself and not judge either one. You are a 64-track recording— the tracks are always there, they're always with you. Sometimes the harsh tracks are cranked up and the rest are rolled down to zero. Other times the sweet tracks are high and the darkness is low. But it's all you.

I came to think that we all have many faces. I always refer to the zodiac. Why do they have all these different creatures to represent different periods in the year? I think it's because those are all the different qualities of a man in different seasons. In the Wu-Tang Clan we took on so many names, identities, and alter egos. But you could also see all nine of us in one person. There's something about me I got from Meth. There's something about me I got from Dirty. There's something about Dirty in every other member. There are all these different identities in each of us.

When I was setting up 36 Chambers studio, I made a point to get eight different compressors—one for each voice in the Wu-Tang Clan. That way, once I found the way I wanted someone to sound, I never had to touch it again. Every time Ghost walked in, there was Ghost's compressor—I'd patch him right into it. That gave it a consistency throughout the album. Today on Ghost's albums, he might sound one way one minute and slightly different the next—because you have different engineers, different compressors, different mikes, different equipment. But at 36 Chambers, I feel I became a part of those MCs' voices and they became a part of mine. I wanted us to have parameters—so you could come in and know who you were, what you'd sound like.

One of my main inspirations for creating a record company and creating my own music was reading about Stax Records. I read the book and I saw how they put up thirty-five dollars to start their record company. I saw how David Porter and Isaac Hayes were sitting there writing all these songs and making all this music and that they used the same band, Booker T. and the MGs with Steve Cropper for many of the hits that went up to 1972. I read this while I was walking and forming my company.

Stax had what? A sound. Motown had what? A sound. Every song was recorded where? At Motown. At Stax. My idea was that every song would be recorded at this place, and I gave it the most obvious name it could have: 36 Chambers. Because that's exactly what it was: the thirty-sixth chamber of my studies—the place I brought my wisdom to the world.

But like most things in life, that chamber had to

close. Right after *Cuban Linx* I went straight into *Liquid Swords,* nonstop. Everyone else in the Clan went off to do their tours, shoot their videos, do their careers. I stayed in the basement to keep working. But soon came the end of that chamber, the closing of that circle. Because right at the end of making *Liquid Swords,* it happened: a flood.

The town houses were built in a group with one drainage system. There was a big rainstorm, and even though I had built everything up a foot off the main floor, the water rose up three or four feet and destroyed my studio. It made me think of that flood back on Dumont Avenue, in Brooklyn, when I was a kid. Water is like that in my life—it brings destruction. And like the kid says in *Shogun Assassin,* from the sample that begins *Liquid Swords*: "That was the night everything changed."

Liquid Swords was pretty much done, but that was it—the studio was gone. In a way it was like the destruction of the Shaolin temple, which caused all the monks to scatter. It was 1996, and I still had to do Ghost's *Ironman,* but I had to do it somewhere else. Even though people like that album a lot, Ghost's voice doesn't sound as good as it did on *Cuban Linx,* because we had to go to someone else's studio to do it—we had to leave Shaolin.

We bought the Wu House in New Jersey and built a studio downstairs there. We built another studio in Manhattan. I made a deal with Sony for twelve million dollars and set up my own company, Razor Sharp Records, also in Manhattan. Then it was time to do *Wu-Tang Forever*. In four years, we'd gone from nine niggas from Stapleton and Park Hill to worldwide celebrities. Wu-Tang Clan was carrying our wisdom from Shaolin to the world.

The world had some wisdom to throw right back at us.

Confusion is a gift from God.

Those times when you feel most

desperate for a solution, sit. Wait.

The information will become clear.

The confusion is there to guide you.

Seek detachment and become

the producer of your life.

CHESS VERSES

THE AESTHETICS OF STRATEGY

Two chess games reveal two styles of warfare. One, the King's Gambit, is nuclear. If you like tactics and violence, that's the way to play. You begin by playing pawn to E4. If your opponent responds pawn to E5, you play pawn to F4, which exposes your king's side to attack from his king's side. If your opponent takes the pawn, he accepts the gambit. Then, the move order that follows is Knight to F3—because he's got to protect the King from check by Queen H5—then you develop your bishop to C4. If you get time to castle, your attack on the F7 square is so immense that the black pieces are going to have to play accurately through the whole game or your opponent will lose. It's not as complicated as a 32-move game, but it is more brutal.

The other strategy is the Spanish Opening, also known as the Ruy Lopez, for the great sixteenth-century chess master and actual Catholic bishop. This style is more like a verse by Rakim. It's deep. There's a lot of theory, it's positional, and the game may go on for sixty, seventy moves. Everything you do is to put yourself in a position for the endgame. It's thirty choruses. With the King's Gambit, you're hoping there isn't going to be an endgame. You're just trying to get this game over fast. A lot of those games end in twenty moves, if somebody's good maybe thirty moves. It's like the Wu-Tang sword style. Immediate, in-your-face—it's on.

THE OTHER CHEEK

A MEDITATION ON KUNG FU
AND CHRISTIAN MERCY

The written characters in the word *Tao* break down in such a way that the word literally means "the Path of the Warrior." A lot of us need to think like a warrior in our lives, even when we're at peace.

A warrior is not simply someone who gets into a lot of fights. A warrior doesn't fight—he kills. When a warrior takes on wisdom, he makes a circle around your punch—he'll lean back to fend off a blow, and if he has to, he'll come back in and kill you. It's a wiser form of fighting, and you see it in all different forms of combat—physical, strategic, military, business.

Jesus said, "Turn the other cheek." That's good advice on many levels. For one thing it takes something out of you to hit a man. It hurts you to do it. But a warrior would take Jesus's advice in a martial arts way. In a street way, it means, if a nigga gonna punch you in the face, you pull back, then come in and fuck him up for real. I've seen this happen to my cousin, Sixty-Second Assassin. A guy tried to punch him in his face, Sixty-Second turned his head, and the fist just slid off him. Also Sixty-Second uses Vaseline in a fight to stay slippery, to prevent contact. That's swift and wise. That's when turning the other cheek becomes strategy, not just righteous living.

If you let a man smack you

in the face, you display power

and grace. But if he smacks

you again? Engage with wisdom

and defeat him. You only

got two cheeks.

GANGSTA CHI

A MEDITATION ON ART AND VIOLENCE

In the mid-'90s, we saw a division of violent music and violent lyrics. In the one case, you had hard-core hip-hop from the East Coast, which had violent-sounding music as well as violent lyrics. But then suddenly, you had West Coast G-funk and music like Biggie Smalls—niggas rapping violent lyrics over smoothed-out beats. The smooth music attracts more listeners—you put sugar in anything, it makes more people eat it. But it changed the public in a strange way.

If the music sounds violent—like "Bring the Mother-fuckin' Ruckus"—that gives the listener a chance to get his violence out into the air. But if you have a violent lyric on a smoothed-out beat, that violence goes straight into your mind. If you're saying, really quietly, shit like "So I saw the motherfucker and I *shot* 'em . . . And I knew when he dropped that I *got* 'em . . .' all with a smoothed-out flow? Over R&B beats? You're not getting it out, you're not releasing that chi. You're getting enticed, the pressure is building.

Gangsta comes in many forms. You can watch a movie like *Die Hard*, which is full of violence that's in your face. But if you watch a movie like *The Godfather*, the violence is subtle—it's in a word, a nod, a gesture. I think you walk out of *Die Hard* and leave something in the theater. With *Godfather*, you walk out with something put in you. Hip-hop is the same way. The smooth gangsta shit puts it into you—which is cool, in a way. But the hard-core shit gets it out of you, and I think that's better. Otherwise, you have it all bottled in—you go to your car, drive home, and kill your wife.

PEACE

The word comes from Islam and is meant to be a universal greeting. It's the only word I use to begin and end each communication with my fellow man. "Peace"—it's the absence of confusion. "Peace"—it's the prevention of conflict. "Peace"—it establishes both parties on a ground of mutual respect no matter who they are. "Peace"—it's universal. If an *alien* jumps in front of your ass—comes at you, like *"BLAAH!"*—you can still say "Peace." He may even understand you.

Peace. The whole energy of the word itself is good.

Peace.

But as they say, come in peace, but prepare for war.

IDEA TRAPS

Wisdom is words, and words are used to trap ideas. But once the idea is manifest, you don't need the trap. When the bear is caught, let go of the bear trap.

DISSOLUTION

How can I put it? Life is like video footage
Hard to edit, directors that never understood it
I'm too impulsive, my deadly corrosive dosage
Attack when you least notice through explosive postage
I don't play, the rap soufflé sauté for the day
Ruler Zig-Zag-Zig A, Leg Leg Arm Head
Spread like plague, we drink Hennessy by the jig
I got the golden egg plus the goose
Eighty-proof Absolut mixed with cranberry fruit juice
Ginseng boost, I got your neck in a noose
Keep my money wrinkled, the rap star twinkle killer instinct
Sixteen-bar nickel sell more copies than Kinko
Grow like a fetus with no hands and feet to complete us
And we return like Jesus, when the whole world need us

—RZA, "REUNITED"

For what does it profit a man to gain the world
and lose his soul.

—JESUS

In 1997, we began to make our second album as Wu-Tang Clan. It was only four years after our debut, but everything was different. For one thing, four of us were platinum-selling solo artists. So the number four came to reveal itself in a new rule. In a group of nine, beware of the number four. If four members are not with you on course, the vessel will not reach its destination.

I knew the only way to record that album was to take everybody away from all the homies and ties in the East. So a crew that helped reestablish hip-hop's East Coast Mecca had to go west. We moved to Los Angeles—stayed in the Oakwood Apartments, started recording at Ameraycan Studio in West Hollywood.

The year was '97—a very serious number in Mathematics. I remember telling everyone that this was the year—the year of 9 and 7, the year of Born God. 9 and 7 is 16, and 1 and 6 is 7. This was a rare year, a rare chance. I even said it in a lyric, in the song "Reunited": "We return like Jesus when the whole world need us." That's how I felt at the time—like we were being called to reunite for the good of the world.

We stayed in Los Angeles for months, recorded the double album *Wu-Tang Forever*, and released it in June. It went to number one in the first week. We were the biggest music group in the world. And that was it; the five years were over. The plan was completed.

On some level, right when that happened, I could feel my power was gone. Even when we were recording the album, I realized the Clan was no longer a dictatorship with me telling who to get on what song and what to do. It had become more free, a democracy. It had to—it was just nature, the Way.

With *Wu-Tang Forever*, we had all fulfilled our destiny. My brothers in the Clan had lived up to their five-year promise, and I had lived up to mine. The planets had aligned, the cipher was complete. There was no more prophesy involved; everything else was gravy. Our future was no longer ordained.

The album dropped in June. By August it was over. Wu-Tang left Shaolin and got lost in the countryside— separated, pulled apart.

It was a tour that did it—with the L.A. rock group Rage Against the Machine. This was my idea. Since we had a number-one album, we could have made more money than we would on this tour, but I felt I was taking the long view. I wanted to consolidate our fans with mainstream America.

Let's just say this wasn't a universally accepted strategy. Wu was strong like a motherfucker on that tour, but backstage, brothers would say, "Yo, why we on tour with these white boys? I wanna go rock with my niggas." I could understand that. They wanted to feel that energy, share that triumph. But I said, "Look, we do the white boys in the summer and do the black colleges in the fall."

Instead, we dissolved. We had the world in our hands and we dropped it. One moment crystallized what was happening: thirty thousand kids holding up *W*s with only three or four members onstage. It was so embarrassing, so totally crushing. The first time that happened was in Cleveland, then there was another disaster in Chicago that involved missing members, violence, police, and the whole nine.

At this point, no one in my crew was hearing me. Method Man was double platinum, Raekwon was platinum, Ghostface was platinum, Dirty was close to platinum, GZA was close to platinum—these were all real stars now, with all the ego, power, and confusion that comes with that. The only ones who weren't to that degree were Deck and U-God, and they were the motherfuckers onstage every day.

One day on the bus, I finally just said, "Fuck this, it's over. I can't do this. I can't keep fronting on our fans and fronting on ourselves." We pulled out of the tour in August, halfway through. And the Wu-Tang Clan scattered.

When the Shaolin temple was burned down, Shaolin was infiltrated by outside forces. In their case, it was the Manchus. In our case, it was money, fame, and ego. In both cases, the masters scattered—some left with intentions to rebuild; others took different paths. Shaolin would survive, but it would never be the same. And neither would I.

For me, this was death—the death of a certain person inside me. If I was the abbot, the leader, that man had ceased to exist. I felt I gave my life to this cause, and that life was in ruins. I'd spent two years living in a basement, and that time changed me. Prince Rakeem was gone. I wasn't that same Polo-wearing cool motherfucker my friends grew up with. Now, I was this Afro-nappy, fang-mouthed Gravedigga–type kid—this monster. In photos of me back then, I look older than I do now. The prince had become a funky-smelling workaholic down in the lab three days straight, not bathing, not eating. I was like Frankenstein, because I didn't care. I thought it was worth it.

Now I wasn't sure. I thought '97 would be the year of Born God, of new birth. But at this moment, it felt like death.

Not only was I let down by the brothers, but my wife betrayed me. She ended up hooking up with another man. I just couldn't believe that. For the RZA's woman to have an affair—how the fuck could that happen? I was heartbroken. In September, after the defeat of the tour, I headed back to my house in New Jersey—a place I'd originally bought as a Wu house—defeated, depressed, lost.

I got there early in the morning on September 7. I'd been drinking, smoking, doing all types of drugs all night long. I knew my family was in the house, but it was a broken family. I couldn't even look at my wife. In fact, I couldn't even get in my own house—the doors were all locked.

It was the crack of dawn, and I went to lie down on the grass. I don't know how much time passed, but after a while something strange happened.

My boy Kinetic was with me, crashed out on the grass, and when I got up, he noticed something. There was a flower there, right where I'd been lying—like it grew under me during the night. He picked it up and showed it to me. I took it in my hand.

I must have looked at that flower for an hour or so— just zoned out, with my spirit doing weird shit, like I was seeing Heaven. All there was, for that period of time, was that flower. It was beautiful, moist, and full of life.

Time passed; the sun came out. Kinetic picked up another flower, tied it in a knot. Then he slid his finger across the flower. You could see that it had lost all its moisture. I looked at the flower I was holding and saw that it wasn't moist anymore either. And then—*bing!*—it came upon me. Enlightenment. And I was free.

In the years since then, I've tried to explain what happened to me that morning. I still don't know if I can. I saw that the flower grew. I saw how the sun causes all things to grow. But I also saw that by noon, that flower was dried out and dead. In a way, I could actually, physically feel the rightness of this—that there's a beginning and end of physical things. It showed me that it was okay this moment had passed. A flower grew under me, where no one would expect it to. It was beautiful, moist, and full of life. Then by noon, it was dry and dead. It had run its course.

I got up off the grass.

I'd been telling everyone this was '97, year of Born God—saying they had to realize the existence of God in themselves. But on the seventh day of the ninth month of '97, it happened to me. I was the one who was reborn. On 6/6 came 36: On June 6, I saw *36 Chambers* on TV—a vision that inspired a style, a hip-hop crew, a rap phenomenon, everything the Wu-Tang Clan became. On 7/9 came God Born, meaning God born into existence, and another vision that freed me—from ego, isolation, and every burden that came with it.

It's a basic hip-hop lesson that's tough to learn. The second you pick up a mike, it's about you. You're telling people who you are, where you're from, how you dominate and control. But Taoism says that to remember the Great Way means to remember your connection with all of creation. It teaches you to harmonize your personal will with the natural harmony of the Way. That is, don't take your car keys and hand them over to your ego. If you do, you'll crash.

On the way up, you do all the things driven by ego. But when you get to your destination, you have to let go of the ego. It's a balancing act you can achieve only if you let go a little bit, act more generously with your time and creativity.

Up to that point, I believed I owned hip-hop. If you read my old interviews, you see it. Hip-hop belonged to me and my crew. It belonged to the East Coast. It belonged to New York. It belonged to the black man. Then I realized something. Hip-hop didn't belong to us. It belonged to the world. In a sense, I saw the larger flow of the world; I saw the harmony in it. I saw that no one could control these forces.

But just because it belongs to the world doesn't mean you should let anybody abuse it. That's the problem. If something is sacred, people want to protect it, keep it to themselves. Jesus said, "Neither cast ye your pearls before swine, lest they trample them under their feet and turn again and rend you." That's why you're so protective of what you think are your pearls.

But Jesus would also say knowledge is free, wisdom is free, you have to give. It's the same thing in kung-fu legends. That's why the Shaolin temple got burned down. Because if you don't care about the outside world and the outside world is full of wolves eating everything up, when they're finished eating everything up, where they gonna go? To *your* crib.

I feel like the abbot knew that, the one I sampled at the beginning of "Reunited," when he says, "I'm afraid disaster must come. We must get more pupils so that the knowledge can expand." In that movie, they start letting regular people into the temple. This brings about the destruction of the temple but the preservation of it at the same time. I feel the same way about hip-hop now. What-ever it will become, it won't do it by being exclusive. And I've felt that way ever since that morning, when I saw the light and changed.

Until that morning, I'd had success, but I was small and twisted inside. Even though I had wealth and fame and knowledge of self, I wasn't free from ego. I was se-cluded, antisocial, aggressive, conceited, and mean. On 9/7/97, I became humble. And ever since then, the person people meet named RZA is all right. Ever since that day, I've been able to talk to people about my life, to tell them I'm not a Muslim, a Buddhist, a Christian, a gangsta, a thug, or a prophet. I'm not any one of these things, al-though in a way I'm all of them. On that day I became me: a humble warrior, a student again. I became free. I found peace. And I've had it to this day.

If you live through defeat, you're
not defeated. If you are beaten but
acquire wisdom, you have won.
Lose yourself to improve yourself. Only
when we shed all self-definition do
we find who we really are.

HIP-HOP KOANS

"Everything is Everything."

When Buddha says "All is illusion," he isn't saying that nothing is real. He's saying that your mind's projections onto reality are illusions. He's saying that the elements in the universe that form every physical thing we see—solid, liquid, gas—if they're taken down to a subatomic level, they don't exist. Therefore all we see is an illusion, because it's shape or form, not true essence. One reason why Buddhism was pushed out was that it seemed to contradict Western ideas of God. To most of us, you can't say "All is void" one second then "Everything has a Buddha nature" the next. But what Buddha said is true.

Your body is your vehicle. And if you put that vehicle to the service of God's will? Then that vehicle becomes an extension of God's hand. This is Moses splitting the Red Sea. This is Jesus walking on water. It's that extension—

because the power of the physical is limited only to the power of the mind and spirit driving or flowing through it. Everything is everything.

"It's All Good."

Both street talk and Zen statement—and true. At the bottom line, at the end of the day, it *is* all good. Even if a bomb explodes and blows up a whole building and all the atoms and matter that were compressed are released, once the explosion is over and things settle back down, it's back to normal again: It's all good. Even though the Devil is causing chaos, from the days of the Bible until now, at the end of the day, God will cast him out. At the end of the day, good will triumph over evil.

Science reflects this. If God is good, if the universe is based on a good energy, all will be good—right down to the subatomic level. Electrons are negative, but they move around the proton, which is positivity itself. It sits still at the center and determines the weight of the atom. No matter what the electron is doing, it's the proton that makes everything what it is. Its weight is something like 1,100 times more than the electron's. The proton is God. It's all good.

"Don't hate the player; hate the game."

That's good street talk, but it makes practical spiritual sense too. It derives from the biblical counsel to hate the sin, not the sinner. In so many words, that's what Jesus said: "Don't hate the player; hate the game." They persecuted him for talking righteousness and speaking the truth, so he just said, "Yo, y'all playin' the game wrong. You're out here living wicked and doing this and doing that, and you're gonna hate me just 'cause I'm telling you about it? Don't hate me, nigga. Hate the situation you're in."

In a way, he even says the same thing to God—which just shows how powerful Jesus's spirit was. He's getting crucified, and in his last moments on Earth, he looks down at his killers, sees they're all pawns in the larger scheme, and tells God to forgive them—because they don't know what they're doing. This is a man who told God himself, "Don't hate the player; hate the game."

"Get in where you fit in."

One of our main problems in life is knowing your place and time. Get in where you fit in. It doesn't mean don't dream and strive for something better. It means that all things manifest in due time. In order for thought to materialize into our three-dimensional world, it takes time. Be patient.

In the Lessons, one question is, "Will you hope to live to see the day when the Gods take the Devil into Hell, in the very near future?" The answer is, "Yes, I fast and pray to Allah to live to see the day when Allah comes in his own good time to take the Devil off our planet." That line "in his own good time" is important. Everything has its own time, its own place.

For example, prophets almost never blow up in their own time. Jesus had twelve apostles—two thousand years later he's got a couple billion. Muhammad had seventy—now it's over a billion. Buddha had five hundred—now another several million. They had to get in where they fit in.

BLING AND NOTHINGNESS

ON FAKE JEWELS AND FALSE PROPHETS

These days, image is everything. But the Bible says to watch out for false images—false images, false prophets, things that seduce us. Consider one fact from the biggest seducer in the United States, Hollywood. No movies use real diamonds. They're always fake. They're false prophets.

You hear rap artists now talk about how their wrist is "frosty" and "frozen" and how "the bling-bling will blind you." Well, maybe it will. Maybe it already blinded you. Rocking too much bling can reveal a hole in a man, an emptiness he's trying to fill with diamonds.

Jewels are minerals, compressed pieces of earth, stacks of crystalline carbon. What gives them shine is their history. It's the same with man. When a man recognizes himself, he recognizes his true jewel, and his body expresses that wisdom. He becomes a jewel himself. If his mind is sharp, the way he walks and talks has a certain beauty about it. Attain wisdom and you have all the bling you'll ever need.

MAN AND ANIMAL

I don't eat meat—I've been vegetarian since 1995. But I didn't stop because I became a Buddhist or a Hindu. I stopped because I had a revelation I was eating dead animals.

It began in a restaurant with one of my students—I had nineteen at that time—and he was eating chicken and I was eating steak. It was Ponderosa Steak House, all you could eat. But some of my students weren't eating any meat at all. In fact, Dirty and I didn't eat meat from ages fourteen to sixteen, but then we started getting into sex and drugs and that led to us being carnivorous.

But this time, my student saw me eating a steak and he pointed to the bone. He said, "Look at that, yo," pointing to the blood on the bone. "You eat that?" And I was like, "Hey, I don't eat *pork,* but I think it's everybody's choice." But something about what this kid said made me reassess. And from that day forth I didn't eat red meat anymore.

I continued to eat poultry and fish. But then one day I was eating a piece of chicken and my teeth hit the bone.

My mind said, "Dead bird. This is me. Eating a dead bird." Like I'm a fucking fool—what, I can't think of anything to eat besides dead flesh? I started thinking about it like, "I'm alive, I have a life, my flesh is alive. Why should I eat something that's dead?" I was still eating fish, but I rationalized that fish is in such multitude that it didn't matter so much. I didn't feel the death of them as strongly. But then I realized they're still all dead—and it felt like the stupidest thing.

I started reading books about it. One lesson I found is called the Great Understanding—it might be by Elijah Muhammed. It said that at one point everything that we ate was alive—we'd eat from the tree, from the ground, our droppings would feed the tree. It was all life and therefore man didn't die. When he put death into his body, he started to die.

From that point on, I ate to live.

SUNSHOWER

A STATEN ISLAND JEREMIAD

Trouble follows behind a wicked mind
20/20 vision of the prism of light but still blind
because you lack the inner, every sinner
will end up in the everlastin' winter
of hellfire where thorns and splinters
pick your third eye out
You cry out your words fly out, and sounds die out
You remain unheard, sufferin' eternally, internal
    external
Along with your wicked fraternal of generals and
    colonels
Releasin' thermonuclear heat that burns you firmly
And permanently upon this journey
Through the journal of the book of life.
Those who took a life without justice will become
    just ice ice ice
It's been taught that your worst enemy can't
    harm you as much as your own wicked thoughts
What devils aught we wrought, and listen naught
Now you're bein' persecuted by that universal court
    court court
I in hell with the strong wine, a fragrant blend of
    sandalwood with rose petals and jasmine
as men use talismans

Burning incense, chantin' witchcraft to reach higher
    dimensions
I'm convinced, Allah is God always has been always
    will be
You could travel every square inch of the planet
    Earth and still be
Ninety-three million miles away from the sun
Till you see you and the sun is one, like the
    knowledge, know the ledge to where your heart is
or fall off into the internal hell that's uncharted
Light travels at the rate of 186,000 miles per
    second through time and space, until it reach
    a target
Now what's the speed of darkness
and show us the path to where the Red Sea was
    parted
Enter ye straight into the narrow gate
for wide is the road to destruction and hate
What you thought, life was a sport?
A game? One hundred years short?
No, the soul is immortal
Going through many portals
and those who go astray
will pay a judgment day
and these few years of wicked bullshit ain't worth the
    eternity inside a sulfur lake
With dragons and snakes
and any pain you can imaginate

Instead, I chose to become a newlywed to the
        true bread
of life and fed God Degree of light to my head
It's been said, the fool who is asleep is already dead
so I stay awake and take care of my brother
and uncover the veil of skin so we can see each other
'cause every color
can make the light appear duller
Who's the colored man? Who's the original?
Who's the biochemical?
Who's the grafted digital, digital, digital, digital
Digital . . .

Two hundred thousand million atoms per cubic feet
        of air we breathe
While niggaz minds are trapped twenty thousand
        fathoms beneath
the sea of reality, they can't inhale deep
devils have 'em stagnant
attracted to .45 Magnums that shatter their bone
        fragments
Cops flood the block you gettin' bagged up by
        Dragnet
Thrown into a six-by-eight steel cabinet
Lifting weights, readin' ancient tablets
back on the block nobody's havin it
Those who haven't learnt get returned

You freaky-ass niggaz get burned
Some walk around like they ain't concerned
with the hell goin' on inside the world
Why do grown men molest little girls?
Is it because the girl's breast has swelled
to the size of a woman, although she's
    twelve
The whole world is sick, sick, sick
Trapped up in six, six, six
I started off as a pawn
in this marathon of life tryin' to carry on
wishin' I had a bomb to blow up Babylon
A vagabond, tryin' to steal clothes from Paragon
Listening to the words of Minister of Farrakahn
Goin' in circles, like a Ferris wheel
Undernourished meals
I cherish hope, drownin' inside the sea of life
Use my third eye for a periscope, and take flight to
    the edge of night
To far heights so dark that even with a bright light
you couldn't see a spark of light
While others play ball, I recall
me and GZA and Dirty hangin in halls, bangin
    on walls
Kickin' rhymes three hours straight with no pause
Boostin' from Freeport sunrise to Amityville malls
Kept razorblade between the jaws, breakin all laws

Started out writin' fables to makin' beats on
  lunchroom tables
to wearin long cables that hung down to my navel
Sold packs of crack and fat sacks of skunk
to bundles of P-Funk, smokin' woola blunts
Dust cocktails and primos
shot more dice than casinos
Back when Wu-Gambinos
were called F.O.I. MCs
All in Together Now Crew B.C.C.
Rec Posse, G.P., D.M.D.
Ol' Dirty stalked East New York GZA maintained in
  Franklin Lane
I was going to Thomas and Jeff, where students
  got slain
Old Earth got nervous brought me to Shaolin sent
  me to Curtis
Took share time in McKee with U-God general
  contractin service
While Meth Chef and Deck was off to New Dorp
  with white boys who took steroids
Buildin' up bicep, tricep, pectoids, and deltoids
Back when our girlfriends was virgins
Cuttin' class with Ghost tryin' to bag hoes in Mary
  Burcham
And Mabel Dean Beacon night school at Washington
  Irving

These young Gods was seekin' hoes in Westinghouse
    and Clara Parton and Medina
Girls who sung like Sarafina
On the corner of Belmont and Picket Avenue
    I seen her
As if I dreamed her
I was dead broke, now I will use key notes to make
    G-notes
So it's always hope
See subway train run through the city like blood
    through the veins
To the heart of Medina, but Shaolin is the brain
So take heed to these words
And feel the power
of the Sunshower

Approaching the final hour
Power equality, Allah sees everything
Let's come together under the wings
And take flight,
Wu-Tang, the saga,
Rzarecta
In your sector

GODS AND HEROES

Not everyone is meant to make a difference.
But for me, the choice to lead an ordinary life
is no longer an option.

—PETER PARKER

It's hard to explain what it's like to be rich, famous, and from the hood. One way is to think of a superhero. Someone who has special powers, a double identity, maybe a secret weakness or two.

Anyone who listens to Wu-Tang knows how deep comic books run with us—how Meth takes the name Ghost Rider or Johnny Blaze, how Ghostface takes the name Iron Man or even Iron Man's alter ego Tony Stark. (It's funny to think how many of our references are in big-budget Hollywood movies now.) Each member could give you a different reason why they chose those names. It's a way to express a different part of yourself. Like how you relate to your favorite movie star, how there's some face you always make and your girl will say, "You look just like so-and-so," and you'll know you do because he's your man, he's part of your identity—his wisdom has filled your vessel, if only for a moment. But alter egos can get deeper as you get bigger. And if you attain fame and wealth, certain alter egos take on a life of their own.

In 1997, my life fell apart, my Clan scattered, my girl of six years and I separated. So I moved out to California and became someone else. I became a superhero because that's exactly how it felt. Think about it. One minute, you're lying in your yard in New Jersey, locked out of your own house—heartbroken, depressed. The next, you're sitting behind a grand piano in a suite in West Hollywood, smoking Cuban cigars with Leonardo DiCaprio right after *Titanic* came out—hearing the biggest star in the world spitting Wu-Tang lyrics at you.

Part of this was a conscious decision that came with awareness of the power I had. For all the years I was wealthy, I sat in the basement and didn't realize it. If you talked to other guys from the Clan about the mid-'90s, they all have great stories and had great times. All I had was turkey burgers, video games, and music. But during 1998 and '99, I made up for lost time. Imagine a man who is free, far from home, and suddenly aware of his powers—that's a superhero. So that's what I became: I became Bobby Digital.

History is full of bad men who redeem themselves to become great. Malcolm X—he came up chasing white women and sniffing cocaine, but found Allah and changed. But what about people who have knowledge and go *back* to doing wrong? For that you usually have to look at our superheroes.

Wolverine: He joins the X-Men and becomes a good guy, but he still goes off by himself for months at a time to raise hell. He was a killer. The man's a superhero, but he'd go into a bar, get drunk, and fuck everybody up in the whole bar. Or even Superman: In *Superman III*, he gets hit by bad kryptonite and it turns him evil and he starts drinking a lot and bullying people. When I saw that Will Smith movie *Hancock,* I almost felt Bobby Digital had to have inspired it somehow. It's about a superhero who drinks, smokes, bullshits around, and doesn't take his responsibility seriously. He's trapped between being a 100 percent good guy and doing bad and no one can stop him.

I did have certain artistic reasons for it. The label Gee Street gave me a big deal to do a solo debut as RZA, and I had planned to deliver a positive, righteous album full of wisdom called *The Cure.* But in order to deliver a record like *The Cure,* I felt I'd have to be living on a mountaintop, a 100 percent vegetarian, deep in some monk state of transcendence. I wanted to be a living example of the words I wrote. But let's just say the time wasn't right for me to do that. In some ways, I was definitely free from this world, but no one would have any idea how I got there or how to get there themselves. So I decided to show the world how I got there, and the only way to do that was to introduce a character who represents my past, my dark hip-hop side. Digi means digital technology on one level, and on a slang level, it means weed dipped in PCP. Both work for Bobby Digital.

A rapper plays a role, but it's different from acting; you really do live that role, almost like method acting. So for Bobby Digital, I was inspired by Robert De Niro— Bobby De Niro. In *Cape Fear* he's a psychopath, in *The Godfather* he's Vito Corleone, in *Taxi Driver* he's an underdog antihero, then in another movie he and Sean Penn dress up as nuns. He's always Robert De Niro, but he lives as Corleone, as Max Cady. I lived as Bobby Digital.

Like a superhero, I had two identities. If you saw me at a party, you'd think I was a party animal. But the next morning, I'd be up studying. I was reading Rumi, the philosophies of Marcus Garvey, all books from the Three Initiates—principles of mentalism, correspondence, vibration, polarity, rhythm—studying genetics—*The Double Helix, The Matrix*. I hung out in the hood in South Central L.A. puffin' weed, smoking sherm sticks, taking mushrooms, kicking it with the Black Knights, which included two Bloods and two Crips. I was teaching them

Mathematics but also exposing them to my lifestyle—they were living the life of a hip-hop star through me, but they didn't even have a record out. The wisdom was pure, but my actions? Not so pure.

I would go hang out with gangbangers but then bring them to my world—parties in Hollywood, huge houses in the hills. I took the Black Knights with me to Ohio and had them all working out, getting in shape, studying, preparing them to be the next MCs for me. But then we went to New York and stayed at the Trump Tower for a month, which I used as a home while recording the Bobby Digital album. It cost me $100,000 for those niggas to stay there, another hundred grand for me—then I had to pay for furniture and rug destruction. We'd hang out on the Plaza's front stoop right by Central Park, watching Patti LaBelle walk in while we're drinking malt-liquor 40s and smoking the fuck out.

Try to imagine it. One second you're hanging out with gangbangers in South Central smoking weed. The next you're headed to London to stay with Richard Branson at his crib in London. One minute you're walking down the street like a regular dude. The next you're rolling in a $300,000 bulletproof Suburban turning your sirens on like you're a cop. One day you're at home in New Jersey having dinner with your family—which I tried to keep together. The next you're in L.A., staying in the Presidential Suite of the Chateau Marmont. You got pounds of weed, bottles of sherm, and you're about to go out to a club with five girls. They're all yours, baby, and two of them are sisters—and I don't mean black girls, I mean siblings. Later you choose which one to sleep with. It's a double life. Hanging with ex-convicts from Staten Island during the day, appearing with John Lennon's son Sean on CNN at night.

In fact, Sean's father went through a period kind of like this—after the Beatles broke up and his marriage was on the rocks. John Lennon goes out to L.A. and flips out—drinking, drugging, clubbing, losing his shit. He hadn't even legally dissolved the Beatles—he was in limbo. I know what that feels like, and I know a lot of people don't come out of periods like that with their mentality intact—they go crazy, wind up drug-addicted, spun out.

I wasn't afraid of that, because I felt free—free to play a role, to have fun, to make up for lost time. But it cost me. All the time I was striving to keep RZA away from Bobby, to keep them as separate entities, but after all the partying and bullshit, I realized one thing. Even though I made the album as Bobby Digital, I made the deal as RZA, so the record company owned the name. I wasn't happy about that. I felt that that name belonged to me and my family—that the RZA should not be owned.

So I went and bought the name back; it cost about $1.2 million. I felt I had to. Bobby was a way to say what I was like when I was nineteen years old and fucking bitches and gun happy. As RZA, I was gonna make my album *The Cure* and live righteously. Bobby Digital was a guy trapped between good and evil. That's how I felt—with all this money, all this knowledge and wisdom, that no one could tell me I was doing something wrong, because I could explain it. I had all this creative freedom, and I just let it run—I let it run like a motherfucker. But you pay a price for that. And in my case, that price was a lot more than $1.2 million.

I'd been living like a superhero, wilding out as Bobby Digital—a master of the universe. Then, in 2000, came my first lesson from this period. On January 9, my moms passed away.

I'd just posed with Ghostface for the cover of the hip-hop magazine *The Source*. That's when I got the phone call. My mom had just died of a stroke, caused by high blood pressure. That day, January 9, I lost my superpowers.

They said it best in *Spider-Man*: "With great power comes great responsibility." When Peter Parker first got his powers, he was a selfish egomaniac; he failed to do right. He didn't give a fuck—he was the man, out wrestling fools, starting fights. A criminal ran by him and he didn't lift a finger to stop him—then his uncle got killed by that criminal. Peter Parker had to live the rest of his life without his uncle. That's how I felt when my moms died.

I remember she gave me one specific order: Never have children outside of your home, away from your wife. Instead, I had kids with four women. That was as Bobby. I'd gone out and put energy and money to places that didn't multiply myself, my people, or my family. And in a way, I feel I paid for that by losing her.

I always knew the year 2000 would bring big change, but I thought it was going to be a change in the universe—I even bought food and preparations for it. I didn't know that the change would be personal. Nothing in this world changed, but in my life, everything did. In the Nation we call our mother our Old Earth. And losing mine—it brought me back to Earth.

I remember getting up to speak at the funeral, and I was surprised by how much joy I felt then, thinking back on our life together. I remembered the nights we had to ask someone for four dollars to get grits for dinner. The night she grabbed me and a butcher knife to go find those teenagers that mugged me. The soul records she'd play—Chic's "Good Times," "Rock Skate Roll Bounce," the O'Jays, Stephanie Mills's "Street Life." Then I thought of the effect one person like her can have on the world.

In the Lessons they tell you not to get tattoos or piercings—not to disfigure your body—but I do have one tattoo: the Wu-Tang logo on my left arm. I felt that I'd give my left arm for this cause. Since then I've seen thousands of those tattoos, if not tens of thousands of them. So at the funeral, I said that my mother didn't bear a family, she bore a nation. Through her children, millions were inspired—to put tattoos on their arms, to make music, write books, create movies—she bore a nation.

But she didn't bear God himself. My life up until then had been making things happen, running shit. With my mom's death, I could feel God telling me something: "You don't control everything." We even learned that in the Lessons: All you control is your own cipher. One lesson it says G-O-D: G is for God, O is for cipher, D is for Divine—God's Cipher (or circle) is Divine. In the Nation of Gods and Earths we call ourselves Gods, but that truly means we're the Gods of *our* own cipher, and your first cipher is first your physical body, the second your family and your home. If someone enters your cipher and submits to your will, if someone joins your crew and submits to your leadership, then the divine union can work. But you have to remember you only control your own cipher. Only God's cipher is divine.

You learn more, you practice more, you gain more wisdom and enlightenment, and you might start thinking that you're God himself. That's because there is some truth to it. If you were to compare to God an ocean, you could say that each one of us has a drop of water in us. In one sense, the drop of water is not the ocean. It's just a drop of water. It doesn't have the magnitude of the ocean itself. But on the other hand, in that one drop of water, you can find the vastness, the magnitude of the ocean. So in that sense, you *are* the ocean.

Digital life proves this. From one bit of a digital image or song, you can reproduce the entire thing. It's the same with DNA. From one strand of DNA, you can clone the whole organism. It's the same with God. From that one drop of water within us, we are, in a sense, the ocean. But never overlook the power of the ocean itself. There's a beginning and an end to what we do because of physical bodies. God is eternal. You will return to him, he's not returning to you. All water in this world goes back to the ocean—it gets drawn up into the sky and goes back to the sea. It's like what Rumi said: "In order for you to become the ocean, you have to drown." If you're swimming, you're not truly it. You have to drown yourself.

My mother's death revealed that truth to me. I came to the hospital, saw her lying there, and tried to breathe life back into her mouth. I couldn't do it. Then I stopped. I thought, *Who the fuck do you think you are?* Then I felt it: I know I'm special, but I ain't *that* special. I ain't Him, the wise prophet that we read about in the Bible (Jesus). At that moment in my life, I became willing to drown myself in that ocean, to submit to Allah's will. At that moment, my superpowers left me. Bobby Digital ceased to be real.

That year, 2000, I learned how much superpowers cost you, what you lose when you let your ego or your alter ego run things. But that lesson came with a second part. That part came a few years later, and it was fatal.

Bobby Digital was an alter ego, but at the end of the day he was a game. I definitely took that game to the extreme. I took it to the point where I was getting ready to roll out at night on some Green Hornet shit: had a suit built for me like the Dark Knight's—literally invulnerable to .45 bullets and knives—had that Suburban, which I called the Black Tank, made AK- and bombproof up to government-security-level standards. I even had a butler almost ready to act as my Kato.

I spent hundreds of thousands of dollars to play this character, but in the end, it was about having fun, about reliving a hip-hop past that got sidelined when I became the RZA. Bobby Digital was someone I created as an escape from the pressures of being the RZA—someone who could rap, act, and even dress in a way that RZA couldn't. He was the kid inside RZA. An alter ego that did not own me. My cousin wasn't so lucky. The kid I knew as Russell, the man I knew as Ason Unique, the artist I encouraged to become Ol' Dirty Bastard—his alter ego consumed him, took the child from him, took him away from all of us. And we just stood by and watched.

I'll never forget the day it happened. It was November 13, 2004. I was with ODB in my studio, 36 Chambers, on Thirty-fourth Street in Manhattan. I brought him there to get him away from the other people around him. He had just missed the biggest Wu-Tang concert, at the Meadowlands, the night before. Clear Channel told us that if everyone in the Clan made it they'd give us a chance to make two hundred and twenty grand apiece. It would've taken only a couple of weeks, and it would have put a quarter million dollars in ODB's pocket for a couple night's work. He didn't make it. He had people pulling him away to do one show for seven grand, another show for five, anything to throw some money in his pocket, let him hang with a bunch of niggas who just let him get high and buy drugs.

That afternoon, I was about to leave him to go do an MTV interview. I went to say "Peace" to him, and I asked him, "You all right, God?" I could see he was bugging out, he'd been getting high for days. That wasn't so new, but I could sense something worse about him this time. Then he did something that made me feel he was stepping over the boundaries of who he was and what Allah meant him to be—and that really disrespected his being.

I have only a slight understanding of why he did this, but he sat his son down and made him watch him do his drugs. His son got up to leave, and ODB grabbed him and said, "No, man. You sit the fuck right here." And I was like, "Yo, I'm out." And he grabbed me with this grip—I should have recognized it; it was the grip of someone drowning—and he said, "You're not going nowhere either."

So his son and I were sitting there, and he was smoking his drugs, and I could feel that he was offending something. He was offending me, I think he was offending his son, and he was offending himself. I had never seen him do this before. Then he showed me something that I pray I never feel, I pray that no one ever feels. He showed me he had lost his vision and all understanding of who he was.

This man was a scientist, a man with vision. Trust me, the man who became ODB, Ason Unique, my cousin, he was a scientist and a minor prophet. This guy could explain anything to you, just from instinct. He had an innate understanding of the world around him. People may not know this from the outrageous character he played, but ODB was a visionary. But he decayed, he lost that vision. In a way, his Bobby Digital phase took over his whole life—it destroyed the man named Ason, the kid named Rusty.

From the time they put him in jail to all the drugs he was doing to all the stress he went through with his family, it took away his ability to see. And this night, he sat there and looked me in the eye and said, "RZA, I don't understand."

That shook me. I said, "What don't you understand? It's simple, God."

He said, "Nah. I don't understand."

I was like, "G, you *gotta* understand. It's real. It's eternal. It's in you. It's there."

And he said, "I don't understand."

Now, I know that right there, right when he said that—we lost him. Eight hours later, ODB was gone.

He left us with two lessons.

The first I never want anyone to forget: When you enter the path of wisdom, of knowledge, of life—don't turn off that road.

Jesus said, "Enter by the narrow gate; for wide is the gate and broad is the way that leads to destruction, and there are many who go in by it." The wide road—that's all around you, it's easy to take, and many people will drag you down it. But find that narrow road, that straight focus, that tunnel of life. When you're on that, stay on it. For ODB to say in his last moments "I don't understand"— that makes me say I don't *ever* want to feel that. I want to always understand. I always want to have faith. But faith can leave you if you don't practice it, don't exercise it—if you let it die inside you. Practice your faith.

The second lesson ODB left us with is just as important. It's about freedom and your cipher—your circle, your family, the people you love.

Death has many causes—violence, scheming, abuse— but a major one we overlook is neglect. We say, "Oh, he's a grown man. He can drink what he wants to drink, smoke what he wants, say what he wants to say." But Martin Luther King said that freedom has its own laws; it's not without its own principles.

You're free to go from New York to Virginia traveling

north and going around the globe. You could do it, but you'd have to travel around the world. You're free to smack someone in the face. You do have that freedom. But they have the freedom to smack you back. That's justice.

I remember thinking about that after I learned the Fourth Lesson in the Twelve Jewels, Freedom. Freedom has a law, and that's Justice. But I don't think I truly understood that until we lost ODB. Equality is the responsibility of every man to one another. If you really want equality and freedom and justice for all, you got to be able to say, "Yo, son. You're drinking too much. You're free to do what you want, but it's gonna kill you."

My cousin ODB died because we didn't pay enough attention. We let him do what the fuck he wanted. I tell my friends now, "Don't ever not stop me if I'm fucking up. If I'm being a dickhead, let me know, please." You have to do that, especially if someone is family. Especially if you love them.

I've even pulled brothers aside on the street and said, "Yo, G, the way you're acting you're disrespecting all of us, man. They're already looking at us as niggers and you're confirming it." Even in a movie theater, like when brothers get excited and yell at the screen. I know that's a big joke about our community, but it's not right. I mean, it's a movie—if it makes you laugh, laugh; if it gets you excited, get excited. But have some respect for yourself and the others that are watching.

My speech at Dirty's funeral was different from the one I gave at my mom's. It was not joyous. I spoke out against everyone in my family including myself. I said that we had all sat there and let a motherfucker we loved be hurting and didn't help him. We allowed this negativity to exist when we knew it was wrong because we didn't want to hurt his feelings. Now we're all in pain.

It's like they said in the Civil Rights movement, if one man is lynching a man in front of twenty men—all twenty men are guilty. They're allowing it. They're guilty of a negligence of righteousness. You have to care for others. There's always someone among you who has to teach those that don't—even if just by example.

There's a statement on a piece of paper that I'd give my girl or my students, a piece of paper I've had since I was fourteen years old. It's titled "Maturity," which it defines as "the ability to change what must be changed, to accept what can't be changed, and to know the difference between the two." That same idea comes up in different sources. It's even in a Mother Goose rhyme: "For every ailment under the sun, / There is a remedy, or there is none; / If there be one, try to find it; / If there be none, never mind it."

It's also in something called the Serenity Prayer, ascribed to St. Francis of Assisi: "God grant me the serenity to accept the things I can't change, the courage to change the things I can, and the wisdom"—the wise-dome—"to know the difference." Again, knowledge means knowing, but wisdom means acting—acting on what you know, seeing the person who's drowning right the fuck in front of you, and stepping in.

My mom's death ripped something from me that isn't coming back. But it forced my mind and heart to remember, to accept what I can't change and get the freedom that comes with that. But ODB taught me—taught all of us—the flip side of that. When we neglect others out of superficial wisdom, fake respect, phony knowledge—we tell ourselves it's their life; we say it's not our responsibility; we don't want to get involved. Fuck that. Get involved. Or we'll all feel the pain.

SOUL

A MEDITATION

Spirit and soul are different. Spirit is an idea, a potential—it's the fire before a match is struck. The soul is a product of God. If man is a mathematical, biochemical equation, the soul is that equation's starting point. It's the dot in the yin or the yang. The soul is that drop of water from God expressed in the flesh.

Drugs can possess you,

but so can your mind.

Learn how to use it,

how to direct it.

Don't give your mind

to a demon.

DIGITAL BRAIN

A PARABLE OF HUMAN INTELLIGENCE

In 1996, a computer called Deep Blue defeated the world chess champion Gary Kasparov. Deep Blue is a frightening opponent but an even more frightening idea—a computer that could beat the greatest chess player in the world, but then Kasparov came back and beat it. There's a lesson in there: A man's thought process can defeat the mathematical calculations of a giant computer—because the randomness of a man's mind is incomputable.

I don't think a computer can process information to even 10 percent of what the human brain does. The brain's got mad shit going on in your body right now. Every cell in your body, even to duplicate one cell—blood cell, skin cell, brain cell—to pump the blood, then reproduce everything every day. It's insane what the brain has to do. Man is supreme.

Even so, the computers are catching up. That's why I feel that man has to become digital. The way things are going with computers and technology, we can't get so that we rely on them completely. We've got to be able to have a concept of digitality within our own selves as well, so that we're always the masters of it.

What man has to do is apply wisdom to his own unpredictability. Right now, man is not always using wisdom. He's letting computers do it. And when a computer can logically outthink a man—that's a frightening step. I've read some chess masters saying that they can do rare pawn moves that seem illogical but will fuck the whole computer up and they end up beating it. I believe they're pointing the way. We must find and use a logic that's not programmable.

DIGITAL CULTURE

ART IN THE AGE OF ONES AND ZEROS

Nowadays, if you say something funny or smart, you'll hear someone say to you, "Oh yeah, what's that from?" And you're like, "I made it up, motherfucker." Sampling, cutting, pasting, referencing—digital culture is so deep in people now that we forget there's such a thing as originality. Many people don't trust a new sound or idea if they don't know where it's "from."

I've even said to myself, *What's the use of making more music when it's all here already?* I may not have discovered it, but it's really already here. Those same twelve notes have been here since the beginning. The combinations may be almost infinite, but it all has the same basic limited foundation. Whether it's being sampled or not, it's the repetition.

I don't see the cultural effects of sampling as being all bad, not by a long shot. But just when options should be more diverse, there's some force countering that, making things more limited. I was listening to some vinyl the other day. I bought a New Birth record, the song "Wild-flower," and I got the MP3 of it too. If you play the two back-to-back, it's insane. They sound almost nothing like each other, even though they're the same song, same recording, same mix, everything. It's reduced, simplified, lost. This generation is missing half the picture.

It's a way of simplifying life—and that's something that you have to do sometimes, for good reasons—but if you do it too much, you lose reality. You risk losing yourself. I believe that what's happening with digital sound and image is prophetic for our culture. With high-def TVs, cable, and everything, our vision is getting sharper. But with the reduction of music to MP3s, at least the way the technology is now, the sound is getting smaller, simpler, blunter. What does that mean? We're getting accustomed to better image and worse sound.

This reminds me of the old movie *Running Man*, where TV producers and the government collude to alter a public news event to make it look as if the heroic rescuer is actually a murderer. In a way, when TV went digital, we lost a foothold in reality. Now, we'll never truly know if what we're watching is real or has been altered and transmitted to us. Digital culture brought a step away from truth.

DIGITAL DJINNS

A CAUTIONARY TALE

They say LSD can induce a consciousness of your connection to God and yourself. I think PCP can too. The
one thing I feel is dangerous about it, as with any drug, is
this: The body is a vehicle to the mind, and if it's a vehicle,
anybody can drive it. So watch what shit enters you. You
might let a spirit in that's not you—like when you see a
nigga and you know that nigga changed.

The spirit of fire exists in the air—it just needs to be
combusted. In the same way, I believe we *will* certain spirits into existence. I know because I had that experience on
PCP where I was truly possessed by a demon.

It was years ago, in California. Digi is PCP mixed with
weed, which is better for you, but this time I did PCP *not*
mixed with weed. PCP is a very powerful thing. All I remember out of the whole thing was struggling for my
life. It felt like fifty people were on me—I saw them, felt
them. Meanwhile, the only people there were me and my
brother Freedom. He was in pain for a month.

The Koran talks about supernatural creatures called djinns—which is where we get the word "genie." They're spirits with their own wills. They have less intelligence than a man but greater physical strength. Some are good, some are evil. I think what happened to me that day was that I exited my mind space into this hallucination world and let something else into my mind space—like a djinn. They said my voice wasn't the same. I was possessed.

NOVICE MIND

A GUIDE TO CREATIVE RESURRECTION

When I started making music, I knew nothing about making music. I didn't know any music theory; I didn't know where C was on the piano. Since then, I've studied music. I've become a Hollywood soundtrack composer, writing music for eighty-piece orchestras. But as soon as I started learning, in 1997, something in me changed. I used my new knowledge to create *Wu-Tang Forever,* but it's not as critically acclaimed. What does that tell you? To me, it tells you to cultivate the novice inside you. Attack each chamber as a novice.

It's important to try new things, things you don't know how to do. With chess, I feel like I might have been better *before* I started studying. I realize that studying has given me a pattern. Before I started studying, I had no pattern—you never knew what I'd do. When I was practicing with a computer recently, I got up to 1650, that's pretty good. That means I have only 350 to go to get to the master level. But I got some advice to study a certain opening—I studied it for a whole year. It was Josh Waitzkin. He's a master, he told me to study this certain opening, and I did for a year. But all of a sudden it seems that I'm using that opening and I'm losing with it. Bad opponents, I wipe 'em out. But good opponents sometimes they'll beat me with that opening.

The opening is called the King's Indian Attack. I know it by heart. I used it against a Sicilian. It goes: 1) E4, the opponent responds C5, white moves; 2) D3, the opponent moves E6; 3) white moves knight F3, opponent responds knight C6; 4) white moves G3, opponent moves G6; 5) white moves bishop G2, opponent responds bishop G7; 6) white castles, opponent responds knight F6; 7) white moves knight C2, opponent castles; then 8) white goes rook E1.

That's the position. The opening I described would be best against the French opening, which is used by many masters. But most club players play Sicilian, which is why I put it in that order. Sometimes it's wise to do an early queen E2, which is a very protective move.

Too many people coast through life, doing only what they know how to do. I always go back to the basics. After Wu-Tang won a Grammy, I began to formally study music—learning theory, how to read music, how to play guitar and piano. But now I try to erase what I know to increase myself. A new piano book I have is called *Beginning Keyboard: Grade One*. A new chess book I'm reading is titled *My First Chess Opening*. It's for kids.

LOVE AND HAPPINESS

It is my fervent hope that my whole life on
this earth will ever be tears and laughter.

—KHALIL GIBRAN

Oh, man, how do I say good-bye?
It's always the good ones that have to die . . .
After laughter comes tears.

—WU-TANG CLAN, "TEARZ"

W isdom is fluid. It brings flexibility and adaptation. It frees you from slavery to your past and
your passions. The wisdom of Mathematics gave the
Gods a kind of balance—it taught us how to carry ourselves when chaos was all around us. The wisdom of
qigong and tai chi shows us how to be a vessel for violent
forces. Today, thanks to this wisdom, I experience emo-

tions like anger the way I experience sex—I let it in and let it out. It's like a thunderstorm; it will pass. I'd been like that for years—affected by the pains of life, but never out of pitch for more than two or three hours at a time. That changed in 2000, when I started losing people that I loved.

When your mother passes away, it takes you years to recover. And just as I was starting to get over losing her, Dirty passed. When I lost them, I lost something I'd had almost my whole life: vision, an ability to see into the future. When my mother died, that vision was cut off. And by 2004, I realized it was truly gone.

When my mother left the physical world, I lost one of my main links to the universe. They say that you have an umbilical cord and an etheric cord, which is the invisible cord that attaches you to your soul, your mother's soul, and all other souls. When one passes away, you really lose something. It's physical and mental; it's real. Part of you dies.

By 2004, all kinds of cords had been cut. I'd lost my moms, we all lost Dirty, I had problems with my relationship at home, and I'd just broken up business ties to my crew: I gave back all the solo contracts in Wu-Tang. Dissipating my company lost me millions of dollars, but it took something even more precious from me. It meant a physical and creative separation of the Wu-Tang Clan, which was also a kind of death. All those separations left me with no sense of purpose, no one to be ambitious for—left me feeling dead and blind.

I was depressed for years. I didn't do much, didn't see many people, mostly stayed in the crib. Then one night, I went out.

I went to a club. It was pitch dark in the spot, and I was in the shadows, physically and mentally. I wasn't RZA, wasn't Bobby Digital, wasn't a celebrity—I was just another dude there in the darkness. And out of no-where, my eyes hit with someone else's and—*bing!*—I got zapped. Right there, I got sparked back to life.

I hadn't been out at night in months; this woman hadn't gone out in a year. This just happened to be the one night we were both out, both in that spot, at the same time. Her name is Talani Rabb, which in the Koran and some African languages translates as "Nourisher of the Heavens." And that's what she was to me. That's what she is to me—we're together to this day. And because of her, in 2005 my vision came back.

I'm not sure why, but I have some theories. In the tale of Samson and Delilah, Samson's strength is in his hair, and when he tells Delilah this secret, she cuts his hair off. He loses his strength *and* he goes blind—literally: The Philistines blind him. Yet at the last moment, his strength is returned to him, he destroys his captors, and frees himself in death. It's a violent story, but it has a profound truth and beauty. Because to me that story is about love.

Samson was blind *because* he was strong—because he was so powerful, he was vain. He wasn't humble enough to really understand God's mercy and will. It took him being blinded and treated as a slave, treated like a dog, to finally, *really* see the presence of God. And with that vision, he became stronger than he ever was before. A woman brought him down—love weakened him—but that weakness showed him a deeper love, gave him true wisdom. Knowledge and Wisdom revealed Love through understanding.

In the most famous story of King Solomon, two women are fighting over a baby. They go to Solomon to settle it. Solomon tells them that he'll cut the baby in half, one half for each. The one who isn't the mother says, "Yeah, good idea." But the real mother says, "Yo, keep the baby." She was willing to waive her motherly rights to the child in order to save his life.

Right there, Solomon uses wisdom to reveal love. When Knowledge (1) and Wisdom (2) come together— that's Love, the twelfth letter. That's the basis for understanding. If you have knowledge and wisdom, you'll understand what love is.

Many men don't understand women, and many women don't understand men. And if you're in a relationship without knowledge and wisdom, you're gonna be dominated one way or another—there won't be any justice. The way to start understanding is to look at yourself. Men and women are not that far apart. Elijah Muhammed taught that 3 percent of a man is missing and resides in the woman's form. This relates to the story of Genesis, where God takes the rib from Adam to make Eve. Adam, who is incomplete without that rib, finds his completion only with Eve. (In fact, in the old Wu-Tang Clan days, we used to call our women our "ribs.") Physically, men and women aren't that different—there's only a 3 percent difference genetically—but that difference creates one of the most powerful forces on Earth. And if you are lucky enough to find that missing rib in real life, that so-called soul mate, the strength built from that harmony is infinite.

That force helped me regain my strength, but after it did things were different. Now I love my woman, but I don't need her like I did. I stay with her by choice. I remember the moment I told her, "I love you, but I don't *need* you anymore." Before, I couldn't live without her. I was so fucked up that if she wasn't there, I wouldn't have made it. But with her mercy I got so I could stand on my own two feet. So I told her, "I was unhappy for years, I really was lost, and if it wasn't for you, I would've been fucked up. And I thank you for that. But I got to tell you that I found myself again and I'm happy. You could leave tomorrow and I'm good. Do not stay with me to help me. Stay because you want to. Because I'm good now."

I know that sometimes you lose your strength, and it seems like it's gone forever. But if you let it, that strength will regenerate. I don't care who you are, if you strive for it, if you wait for it, if you got the mercy to live to see that day, it will return. In 2005, my mind rebooted. The numbers in 2005 add up to seven—another God year—and in that year I feel someone pushed reset, and I came back to life. And I believe that same force is alive today in the world. Right now—like we're all ready to be zapped back into life.

In a way, we're resurrecting ourselves. Commentary like the *Haditha* says, "The first soul that Allah made was the soul of Muhammad, and from his souls all other souls were made." They say that his soul enters a body—anybody's—when it is needed. It's like Neo in *The Matrix*—just by existing he frees all humanity. It's like Buddha—they say his soul waited thousands of years to be born. What this tells us is that energy is always there, waiting to be born. And the people bring it into being—through our will, our pain, our need. We call what we need into being—to spark us all back to life.

For example, I believe we brought into being Martin Luther King Jr.

Years ago, I was like a lot of brothers who grew up militant in the hood; if I had to choose between Martin Luther King and Malcolm X, I'd always go with Malcolm.

But when I was sixteen, I heard one of Martin Luther King's speeches—about the chemical makeup of a human being. He said that scientists had broken man down into his base elements. They found he has enough iron to make a penny, enough zinc to make some nails, enough fat to make a little soap, etc.—all of it adding up to twenty-eight dollars' worth of chemicals. Therefore, there's something intrinsic about man that makes up his true value, something beyond this physical compound. When I heard that speech, I realized Martin Luther King Jr. was a scientist, a blessed man. He gave the "I Have a Dream" speech—maybe the greatest speech of all time—when he was thirty-four years old, and worth twenty-eight dollars in raw chemicals. But his spirit was priceless. He died five years later, at thirty-nine. We brought him into being because we needed him.

In a way, I believe this generation called Barack Obama into being. This moment was prophesied. Even in the Lessons, it says that the world was given a seventy-year grace period, from 1934, until an Earth-shattering change would come. Seventy years after 1934 was 2004—the year of Obama's first speech at the Democratic Convention. In that speech, he referred to his name, Barack, saying that in his father's language it means "blessing." And I think he really is a blessing for our country.

Or look at the numerology. Obama is the 44th president. 4 and 4 is 8—which is the number that represents Build. That was his message to terrorists at his speech before the Lincoln Memorial. "You will be judged by what you build more than what you destroy." He is here to build. But the numerology holds even if you consider the fact that, although he's the 44th president to be sworn into office, he's actually the 43rd man to hold the position—since Taft served two nonconsecutive terms. 4 and 3 equals 7—again, the God number. And Obama won on the 200th anniversary of Lincoln's birth. 2 represents Wisdom and 0 is cipher—it's Wisdom making huge change in the world. I believe that wisdom will save America. For many years, people around the world were aiming missiles of hatred at us, and the Obama presidency has already begun to change that. Someone asked me what happens if he messes up as president, but I say that Obama can't mess up. He's already made the change just by being elected. A century ago, man didn't think he could fly. Once the Wright Brothers first got twenty feet off the ground and went a hundred yards, that was it. It inspired the whole world—to the point that motherfuckers are shooting shuttles into space. That's what Obama did for us as Americans, as a people. He released the shackles off our minds, he released possibility.

This is the hip-hop generation, and that generation now has a black president. To me, that means it is time for us all to be men. Not to be kids, not to be boys. It's time to recognize the true value in a man—aside from his loot, his color, his chemistry. And to realize that each man has that same value, that same potential within him.

Since I'm known to be a student of the Five Percent, people know I was taught that the white man is the Devil. But I believe people misunderstand the practical application of that wisdom. It relates to what Jesus said about the flesh being weak. Yes, I believe the white man has a nature he must contend with, and historically, that nature has been aggressive, violent, conquering, and prone to devilishment. But to me, there's a simple explanation for that. If you have a birth record of six thousand years on a planet that's trillions of years old, with people who've been here for millions of years longer than you, you're a baby. You just need to grow up.

So I wouldn't categorically say that the white man's a Devil, the black man's a God, the woman's an Earth. I'd say those attributes are in their nature, but that everyone can choose what nature they express. They can change. It also says toward the end of our lessons that any man made weak and wicked is a devil. That applies to black, brown, red, yellow, or woman. We all have to change. Think of what the Reverend Joseph Lowry said at the end of Obama's benediction—his last line: "It's time for white to embrace what's right." Yo, G, that's a bold statement. He's saying that to the world—the whole world's watching. To me, that's a challenge to all of us.

Some forces will always fight change, deny resurrection. Some people see someone like me—someone who used to be a thug, an outlaw, and has changed—and they'll get mad. Even in my own crew, we got a dispute behind this. Raekwon will be like, "I wanna make music to punch niggas in the face, and RZA's on this peace shit." Nah, man. I found peace and I'm sharing it.

I *am* from that era in hip-hop, the era of violence and attitude. I helped found that shit, because that's how I felt at the time. I don't repudiate it. But at the same time, all that aggressive, ignorant, nigga-ghetto shit isn't naturally me. It was a product of history and my environment.

Man himself, outside of history, is made in the image of God. God ain't no nigga. God ain't no stupid mother-fucker. God is a prince. Being a killer is not naturally in any of us. I don't even think lions are natural killers—it's like the taste of blood came later. If you believe in the Bible and you go to the Garden of Eden, every animal was there. They were all chilling—there was no death going on. You have to think that death and killing came from an evil nature loose in the world.

Of course, you see that nature everywhere today—sometimes in people repping God. Islamic terrorists would say they sacrifice their lives for God—they're doing God's will. But we're talking about bombs blowing up markets, planes crashing into buildings—is that the work of God or the work of man? To me, it's simple. These men not only kill thousands of others, they also kill themselves. The prophet Muhammad says, "Whoever kills himself with a blade will be tormented with that blade in the fires of Hell." God wants you to live. If we know nothing else about God, we know that. In fact, I don't even believe God wants us to die.

Opposites are not always in a partnership. They are not always like yin and yang, two sides of the same coin. I don't believe that life and death have a partnership. I don't believe that we *have* to die. I believe that we make ourselves die.

I don't deny the force of decay, the depletion of your energy. The second law of thermodynamics says that all physical systems get more and more disorganized over time, until they reach a state of equilibrium. It says that time goes in one direction toward chaos until the system is balanced. I bear witness to that. I just believe the system is bigger than most people think. Energy or even matter cannot be destroyed, only changed in form. So where is death?

See, I believe death is the biggest hustle there is. It's the biggest scam—because you can say what you want about it and nobody can prove you wrong.

The main scam is that you have to die to go to Heaven. This was a strong force in the black community—people put up with anything if they think they're going to Heaven. Or with the Arabic jihadists—being promised gardens and wells because they're in the desert. You promise people what they lack. It's a good hustle. Jesus died for our sins, and through Christ we'll have everlasting life. You can't prove it wrong or right. Death is the biggest trick out there.

But what death truly is is a depletion of a form of animated energy. It's like what happens with a wound, which makes your chi unable to connect; it's like a wire cut in a toaster. So I don't believe death has a partnership with life. Decay is inevitable, but death is not.

Physically, yes, all things decay. But we overlook man's power of regeneration, which comes from a fundamental will to live. I believe that every cell has this spark of intelligence in it, just as every cell has DNA in it. I think everything *wants* to live—down to the microscopic level. When you physically die, you get maggots, germs, bacteria—all the other life-forms that are in your body, that your cells are fighting every day begin to manifest and grow and take form. It's only when the de-animation of your whole organism happens that they get a chance to grow big enough to have a life of their own. Something is always trying to consume you.

There's a Wu-Tang teaching that says when you're about to physically pass away, when your body is about to lose its last energy, you can take your last breath and your last thought and take yourself somewhere else. Your body is a vehicle, like a car. If it's out of gas, if it's out of energy, if it no longer works—get out. Get another one or walk or put it in neutral and push it to a gas station. I look at life like that.

The Lessons taught us that the seventh plane of energy is consciousness or infinity. Infinity is a natural plane of our energy. That's where you are super-conscious. I think you can, at that moment, make a choice. At the end of your body's physical life, when your physical animated energy's running out, you'll know it. Even if it's one second, it won't feel like one second—because it's like being in a car accident when you witness time stop—your mind is going to erase time for that second. This wisdom is also reflected in the Tibetan teachings that guide you through that moment of consciousness between death and rebirth. You have a moment when you can go wherever you want to go, do whatever you want to do. Use that moment.

I was telling my children this. I told them, "If we love each other like this, I don't ever not want to see you again. I want to love you forever." And the only way to do that is to have such a strong love that it exists even without our physical bodies. I know that my mother's not here anymore, but I don't feel she's gone in death. I know I'll never see her walk into my kitchen, but I don't feel that she's dead. Her body is dead, but she can't be dead because life is eternal. And I still see her in my dreams and in places we never visited in our physical lifetimes. When we say something is alive, that's an adjective describing a state of matter. So being alive doesn't actually mean having life. Life is beyond the scope of our natural dimensions—it transcends the duality of dead versus alive.

Back at 36 Chambers Studio, I started doing something I learned from another producer, D.R. Period. He arranged every one of his records by year and category. So when he wanted something from 1972, he'd just go right to 1972. When he wanted horns by Chuck Mangione, he'd go right to horns, 1976. So that inspired me to keep all my horns here, all my female vocalists over there, all male groups there. Now I have a new section: all the great brothers who passed away—like Donny Hathaway, Marvin Gaye, John Lennon, Isaac Hayes. And it hurt me, the day I put Dirty in that section.

But it's the same with Dirty. I know I'm not going to see him again physically. But you're going to hear him and see him for the rest of your life in one form or another—from his music, or from somebody saying something about him, or from a story or a memory. I have dreams about him sometimes, and in my dreams he's actually with me—we're chilling and drinking 40s, doing what we do. And the dream feels like ten years of lifetime.

I lost my vision in 2000, and truly knew it was gone by 2004. But in 2005, it started to come back. And later that year, in September, it came back full force. It happened when my son was born, in September of 2005, the moment I saw him come out of my wife.

It's funny. I thought back to the time I saw my first daughter come out, back in 1992—how that inspired me to get my life together, to form Wu-Tang, to take on the world. But witnessing that whole process again, witnessing that burst of love in my wife and my life—that hadn't happened to me since 1992. But this time, that experience, that seed coming out—it brought me back. It restored my vision for good.

In the Lessons, of all the Twelve Jewels, the last one you get is Happiness. You attain Knowledge, Wisdom, Understanding, Freedom, Justice, Equality, Food, Clothing, Shelter, Love, Peace—*then* you're happy. But there's one crucial detail about happiness missing from the Lessons we were taught, something I learned about only recently.

When the Father founded the Five Percent, he compiled the Lost-Found Lessons and gave them to the youth, but for some reason, he took the first page out. I didn't learn this until Wu-Tang was on tour the first time after ODB had passed away. That was when I actually got a copy of the intro to the Lessons. It's right on the first page, one most Gods never saw. And what it said was this: "Set yourself in Heaven at once."

When I read that, I realized, "That's it." That's the central message of all wisdom—not just in the Nation of Gods and Earths, but of all wisdom: Set yourself in Heaven now. Immediately. Set yourself in Heaven—*right now.*

You don't have to die to go to Heaven. Heaven is on Earth. If you're fucked up, if shit is floating by you, if poverty and self-hatred are breaking you down—you're in Hell. Set yourself in Heaven at once. When Jesus said that the Temple of God is in you, he wasn't speaking metaphorically. He said, "Thy Kingdom come *on Earth as it is in Heaven.*" Many people misinterpret that. The true meaning of that prayer is the same as the Buddhists' idea of Zen, of finding Nirvana and enlightenment right now. The key is true consciousness, in the present, in this moment, right now, where you're at. Don't wait for it. Set yourself in Heaven at once.

Strive for the super-consciousness that comes at the end of life—strive through meditation, through love, through building, through creation. Ignore the forces of darkness, separation, and death. Tune out the voices that don't want you to grow, to change, to resurrect yourself. Ignore forces pulling you back into the past.

It's funny. In hip-hop, people have been talking about "back in the day" for about twenty years now. But that's something people do in general. Your father says, "In *my* day . . . ," his father says, "In *my* day . . . ," and before you know it you're slaves—literally, in the case of black people, spiritually in the case of everyone. You're slaves to the past, to nostalgia. You're blind to what's right in front of you.

To me, Gladys Knight said it best, in the song Wu-Tang Clan sampled for "Can It All Be So Simple." In the part you hear in the song, she says, "Let's talk about the good old days." That's the part everyone remembers. But in the rest of that song, she says something else. She says, "These days now that we're living will become our children's good old days." There's real wisdom in that.

It's like Rumi says, "Past and future veil God from our sight; burn them both up with fire." Nostalgia is self-gratification for those who were there. It's not a statement of the truth. So fuck back in the day. Open your eyes to what's right in front of you. You're here, now, and God is within you. Every day is a good old day.

Some people say, "God works in mysterious ways." But I don't think God is mysterious. In fact, the attributes of Allah don't even include the word *mysterious*. Benevolent, merciful, all-knowing, all-seeing, omnipotent—yes. But mysterious? Nah, he'd say, I'm obvious. I'm everything that you see. I'm right there in front of you. I'm inside of you.

This year, I have my vision back. I can forecast the future. But I don't forecast forming a brotherhood, waging a war, starting a movement. All I forecast is good, because that's all I see. In 2005, I had a son. I named him Rakeem because in a way he was the rebirth of me. His birth—the love it sparked, the strength it gave me—made my vision even stronger. But the main thing it let me see was the presence of Allah in everything.

On the latest Wu tour, I started to say this, plan that, make all kinds of predictions—then I caught myself. I

said, Nah. I'm not in the future-predicting business anymore. All I predict is good. Even where others get stuck on
the *illusion* of bad, I'll be waiting in the midst of the good,
waiting until the aftermath of the bomb or the storm,
because that's when all returns to calm. That's where
you'll see me, building strong, living in the world Allah
manifested.

THE MEANING

The meaning of life is easily stated. <u>L</u>ive. <u>I</u>slam. <u>F</u>or <u>E</u>ver. Islam is peace, so what life truly means is, "Live in peace forever."

Peace.

THE
UNIVERSAL CHANGER

[WRITTEN BY DIVINE PRINCE MASTER RAKEEM
AT 64 TARGEE STREET, STATEN ISLAND,
AT 10 P.M., JULY 4, 1989]

Peace. As we know, all elements radiate a form of energy. Fire radiates heat, ice radiates cold, and man radiates thoughts. Some thoughts are created, others are duplicated and modified. God is the creator of thoughts; the Devil is the duplicator or impersonator. Yet God and the Devil both change thoughts. God changes stories for the better, the Devil for the worse.

It has been said that any thought conceived can be expressed. These expressions of the thought are dormant. It has not the qualities of good or bad. It is neutral. It is a potential energy awaiting to be activated into the kinetic. Yet once it is activated, it takes on the expression of whichever degree it is manifested in. For one may feel that he has a positive thought, but if he expresses it wrongly, it becomes negative. Because sometimes what is positive and good for the individual may be bad for the group—and vice versa. So from this application, we can see that our personal thoughts must be mastered and executed correctly. There are approximately five billion people on the Earth, and they all have the power to radiate thoughts. Yet out of all these different thoughts, there is only one truth. Although all men have their own thoughts of what, where, why, when, and how. And they also manifest ideas of who, if, and but. Regardless of these billions of thoughts, there's only one truth. Everything else is an illusion.

An example of this can be shown through simple mathematics. One plus one equals two. Meaning, one object plus another object equals two objects. That is the truth in any language. This can be shown and proven, and mathematics cannot lie. It is the language of God. So that no matter how many thoughts exist there is still just one truth.

When a man lies to the next man, who is really being played for the fool? For the truth always reveals itself in its own good time. And a lie is only an illusion. For even when you lie to someone, he or she might not know the truth, but the applicator of the lie knows the truth. And that shows that the truth always exists and a lie is only a temporary illusion that vanishes once the truth is manifested.

Nowadays, it seems that the world is confused and filled with chaos, disease, famine, war, hate, poverty, and devilishment. In these days and time, the Devil is in full control and we are living in physical hell. The world is filled with lies and illusions. Billions of people are living in illusion—they are mentally blind, deaf, and dumb. Yet each possesses the qualifications to build or destroy. Our thoughts are the governing, dominating power on this planet. Each thought is like a bomb. It could either save you or kill you. It has been said that words kill faster than bullets. Yet both words and bullets are created by thoughts. In fact, all you see around you comes from the thoughts of people. So who can man blame for the condition that the world is in besides man? Who can change the world besides man?

As I look at this world, I see that it has become a place of sexual perversion, violence, drug abuse, disease, etc. Yet if we look at each of these things individually we can see where they come from and who is causing them to happen.

It can be shown and proven how one thought can change the world for good or bad. If we look into the first book of the Bible, Genesis, we see where negativity started. First Eve eats of the forbidden fruit, so the first sin is committed. Cain killed his brother Abel, so he was the first murderer. Ham looked upon Noah while he was naked—this became the first perversion of thought. Canaan was cursed with disease, thus disease was born. There are many more names and events in Genesis where sin begins. Each unrighteous act took only one thought from one man or one woman. Everyone else took on these actions. They say that Eve was the first to sin and from this all sin was derived. Genesis is the first book of the Bible and Revelation is the last book. It took only one sin and one thought to put the world into hell. So maybe it would take only one thought to change all this. Just as if the president expressed the thought of going to war, we'd go to war, so it only takes one thought of peace to bring peace. This one thought must be properly manifested through the righteous will. So out of six billion people, one man or woman may have that one thought that may change the world. Yet in order to change the world, one must first change oneself. As the popular song goes—look at the man in the mirror. Once man destroys the Devil in himself, he will be able to conquer Hell. There are many people who say that you can't change the way things are, but they are wrong. If God created thoughts and the Devil duplicated thoughts, and both have the ability to change the outcome of thoughts, God thought to create a world of beauty while the Devil duplicated his thought by building his own world. God thought to make a world of peace, while the Devil made a world of war. Thus it is now up to man to change it back. God and Devil both are only man. Man made the world what it is, and only man can change it. So don't be deceived when they tell you that you can't change things, because you can. When you are hot, you jump into the water to become cool. When you are wet, you lie in the sun to become dry. That's a minute example of the power of change.

The first step is knowledge. You must know what must be changed. And the only way to know this is by looking at yourself and knowing yourself. A good man will see the goodness in himself and the devilishment in the world and so will attempt to change the world to good. Yet in these days, everyone has some type of devilish thoughts inside. So he must first change his thoughts, then change the things that make him think in that devilish way or avoid them. Then he should start teaching people the right way to think. How can you tell what is the right way? Simple. There is only one right way and that is the truth. Although some may approach it from different points on the cipher, they still arrive at the same truth. For one plus one equals two anywhere in the universe. In order for one to find God, he must first look inside himself. Thoughts are the key to life, just as a man thinks them. One thought can change the world. So, brothers and sisters, don't let the Devil tell you that you can't change things, because you can. The only thing you can't change is the truth, for the truth is that which in times changes things back to their original state. Right now we are living in illusions. Five billion people are living in illusions. And out of all these people, only 5 percent advocate the truth. They are the ones who will produce the thoughts of a change. And out of this 5 percent may come one person with the perfect solution. It could be you, it could be me, it could be your child, your son, daughter, brother, sister, etc. But that one will be the universal changer. For the ability exists in all of us. So first clean your own house, and then you can help us clean the five billion other houses. And God will show and prove that he is the Universal Changer.

Peace.